SECRETS
OF A
SURPRISING
GOD

To Greta
and Annie
and Kelsey

and all the rest of God's children

SECRETS
OF A
SURPRISING
GOD

JOSEPH J. JUKNIALIS

CROSSROAD • NEW YORK

1990

The Crossroad Publishing Company
370 Lexington Avenue, New York, NY 10017

Printed in the United States of America
Typesetting output: TEXSource, Houston

Library of Congress Cataloging-in-Publication Data

Juknialis, Joseph J.
    Secrets of a Surprising God / Joseph J. Juknialis.
      p. cm.
    ISBN 0-8245-1073-9
    1. Church year meditations. 2. Catholic Church—Prayer-books and
devotions—English. I. Title.
BX2170.C55J84 1991
242'.3—dc20   90-45011
                                          CIP

Contents

Introduction

MORE YEARS BACK than I should care to admit or remember there was a pop song on the charts with a line that went something like, "Scratch a tin god and you'll find a fallen idol." Scratch this world, however, and what you find is none other than an ever-present God. Indeed, there is only one world — this one. There is only one kingdom — this one. There is only one place to find God — in this one. The difficulty is that God looks too much like this world. And maybe that is what Jesus was or is all about — letting us know that there is the vision and the reality. Ours is indeed the story of the two who were crucified with Jesus — one able to see and daring to hope he might share in that which is beyond death, and the other not even able to fathom the question. Isn't that us all — bouncing back and forth between the crosses on which life has hung us? And the mystery is that God is there among them and hanging with us.

To experience life is to experience God. And whether or not we recognize that as such doesn't matter a great deal — unless of course one does not mind failing to discover one is loved. Nevertheless, there is no other life. There is no other God.

However or whenever we come to discover that gift, God is there all the time, playing among those times *before* we have come to see so clearly and tucked among those times *beyond*. And in the end we find God slipped *in between* as well — all too surprising to be believed. That is what this book is about — a scattered collection of such discoveries, all *secrets of a surprising God*.

Part One

A TIME BEFORE—
of Advent & Christmas

1

Shoots of Tomorrow

"THE DAYS ARE COMING," says Martha who lives next door, "when those kids of mine are going to have their own kids, and then their hair is going to turn gray, just like they're doing to me. That day'll come — you just wait," she says with an eager smile.

And some time back, along with George Bush's presidency, came a new crop of Democrats as well. And they came not without their own crystal ball. "The days'll come," they promised, "when George Bush is going to have to raise taxes. You just wait and see. Those days'll come."

And my brother keeps telling his little girl, "Stop wishing your life away," as she keeps wishing it was already Christmas (or, in different times, summer vacation or her birthday). "You're going to grow up all too soon," he says. But she doesn't seem to recognize it. Except she will, some day.

Life is filled, it seems, with hints of what's to come, with shoots of tomorrow breaking through today's barren crustiness, with promises that other folks make for us and we end up having to live with all the way into fulfillment. It is much like Martha's mother saying once long ago, "Just you wait till you have kids who turn your hair gray." And then it happens — not all at once, of course, except that we recognize it all at once, recognize what has been going on inside of us and around us for months and maybe years. It is Martha having to live with her mother's promise, and George Bush who has had to learn how to live with a Democratic swami, and my niece growing up and wondering when it happened and how her father knew it would, and not being able to grow young.

Strange, too, why it is that we always miss those shoots, those promises of days to come. It may very well be that we want to miss them, that we do not want to notice them, for then we would have to live our lives differently — more responsibly or more cautiously or maybe just more honestly.

The days are coming, says the Lord, when the yellow brick road will go right past the front of our house — when we will be wiser (though also older), when we will go with the flow (though not without having tried to swim up current), when people will be treasured more than things (though we will have already sampled the latter).

Those days do come, and the shoots do blossom into divine fruition, but not without some of our stars falling from their high places. It always seems that there is room for only one universe at a time, and before a new universe can come to be, the former must be dismantled or unraveled or whatever it is that is done to our worlds and suns.

There is a friend of mine who is a devotee of backgammon, so much so that he will go to tournaments around the country. I asked him the other day what it is about the game that makes it such a challenge, for to me it seems to be just another kind of checkers — "more luck than skill," I have thought. He went on to explain to me then how there are different levels of play and understanding, of skill and calculated risk, and how, in order to move on to the next level, players have to totally unlearn the principles they have come to trust at the current level. He spoke of how in the last two years he had made that journey, and how only in the last three months (after twenty months of blindly trusting the process) had he come to sense that the new way was indeed better and more skillful. He said it all with a sound in his voice that seemed spiced with a touch of anger, as if to know that the entire relearning was not yet complete, but only the shoot of more dismantlings to come.

The days are coming, says the Lord; and they do come, just as he promised, but without tinsel or miniature Italian lights and not to the tinkling sound of sleigh bells, and never with a "Ho! Ho! Ho!" The days do come, but they come quietly and even out of place like a shoot of Davidic springtime in the middle of winter. They

do come, but never noticed until the deed is done, like wrinkles of
wisdom etched by life upon our brow.

The days do come when, amid life's struggle and anguish and
pain, we are finally remade into the most marvelous of images —
into the image of our God. And we never even knew it.

> *the days are coming, says the lord, . . .*
> *in that time*
> *i will raise up for david a just shoot;*
> *he shall do what is right and just*
>
> *jeremiah 33:14–16*
> *advent*

2

Pretending Other Worlds

STRANGELY (AND YET NOT SO STRANGELY) our "without's" do shape and form our "within's." Sunday-go-to-meetin'-clothes do more to subdue original sin in a child than does a cascade of baptismal water. Smiles — curiously enough — change the color of a room, even when they are forced. And titles, to our dismay, bestow importance, but also, to our amazement, reveal the gift of self-worth — especially when the spirit's piggy bank is empty.

When I was in college we had a professor who would often say that if, instead of acting the way we feel, we would act the way we would like to feel, then we would soon begin to feel the way we hoped to. And, at least for me, life has canonized his wisdom. When robes of mourning and misery are exchanged for robes of glory, transformations do take place. In other words, smiles do change dispositions and titles do affect self-concepts. Now I understand that they are only robes, no more than cover-ups; and cover-ups are never meant to do more than mask the reality, never really change what is. And yet, somehow they do.

We who trek into Christmas carry with us a year's baggage as well. We come with good memories and moments peaked with joy, sun-stretched summers and dappled autumns, vacations that drained our stress and at times even our energy; but we also make our way into this red and green season with a generous share of hurts and pains, failures, and even sins. Most years end glazed bitter-sweet, simply because most years are lived in such a way, the whole year through.

14

And so during the last month of every year, before the calendar gets filed among the diaries of another year, we robe ourselves with joy — we play at being happy and pretend that all is good. We sing carols and toast friendships and wish each other blessings of goodness. And we do it all with an unspoken honesty, knowing full well that life is not always so; but maybe by pretending, a robe of joy can fill the valleys and smooth our personal roughage and, by some freakish twist of Godliness, make the unreal real.

Of such stuff is conversion and repentance made. It is a decision to be other than what we are, even before it comes about, even before we know that it can be. Yet we begin by saying we will be new — a kind of pretending, if you will, for what we seek to be is not yet. But the choice (the new robe) becomes not only the first step but the means as well, and reality too.

Thomas Merton once wrote (though I couldn't tell you where I saw it — as often as I have gone looking) that we always become the people we want to become. And it is true. It does happen. People who seek power do wield power — at least in their own fiefdoms. Those who hunger for wealth, if nothing else, do become greedy. Those who value honesty do in time become honest. And those who hope to become patient, or merciful, or wise, do become such. We do become the kind of people we want to become.

Like a mime robed in whiteface who begins by pretending another world and then suddenly and perhaps frighteningly discovers another "me" released within by the mask, conversion in much the same way masks and unmasks. And it does so in time, a time not calendared or clocked, but tick-tocked by the spirit within us.

During the presidency of Richard Nixon we found ourselves converted to pacifism (perhaps robing our fears with a chosen need for conviction). In another time, consciously aware of our own prejudices, we nevertheless chose to stand for equal justice for every American, and we chose that stance in time — during the strained 1960s or the indifference of the 1980s. When we are face to face with an unwanted pregnancy, it is in that time that we are called to make the ultimate choice as to whether or not we will choose life. And it is only when addiction is translated as death that we grudgingly choose the opening to freedom. And it always takes place in time — Richard Nixon's time or Ronald Reagan's time, married-time or single-time, in health or in illness, in fear or in challenge. It is in time that we become the kind of people we choose to become. And it begins, always, with a first step — a kind of pretending when old robes are exchanged for new.

> *jerusalem, take off your robe*
> *of mourning and misery;*
> *put on the splendor of glory from god forever:*
> *wrapped in the cloak of justice from god,*
> *bear on your head the mitre*
> *that displays the glory of the eternal name.*
>
> *baruch 5:1–9*
> *advent*

3

The Gift of Fear

C HILDHOOD WAS FOR MOST OF US a collection of worlds. Side by side, those worlds seldom seemed to have any effect upon one another except at the edges. There, where they touched, we crossed over from school to home to play. But beyond those crossing points, there was little exchange between them.

There was one world, however, that had only nighttime existence and very defined boundaries — the twelve inches of space beneath our bed, the fifteen square feet of closet space, and the attic. It was a bedtime world where monsters and ghouls prowled our darkness and our fears. Though no one actually ever saw such dust ball denizens of storage and closet, and though no child ever admitted he or she lived and slept with such suspicions, has there ever been a child not plagued by their pursuit?

Somewhere along the way into grown-up, however, we exchanged our worlds for others of different mixings — school for those of work, toy cars and doll houses for suburban models of both, and playtimes for playtimes with different games. Fears, too, we traded, exchanging one closet for another and coming to realize that those monsters that once lived beneath our beds now live beneath our hearts. The truth is that we adults are as fearful a gathering as we were as children — and perhaps more so.

Fearful of admitting our fears, we find ourselves forced to redefine courage as well. With Superman as a role model, we emulate that fearless man of courage and steel, forgetting that courage without fear is never courage — perhaps powerful might or ignorance of foolhardiness, but never courage. Courage is only so in the face

17

of fear, a willingness to stand despite the panic propelling us to flee. Though we are hesitant to admit our fears, courage becomes real only in the presence of those fears.

The media of our society so often continue to distort such courage, transferring such awe to the world of sports. And so we speak of a team that produces a great comeback as one with great courage, and a hero who plays despite pain as a person of notable courage. It is a sad reality that as a nation without war we have come to be hard put to find national leaders of courage outside the arena of sports. And as a result we seldom speak of heroes and heroines except in that arena. Yet what propels the athlete is not courage. It may be drive or determination or a desire to win — but hardly courage.

Perhaps more than anything else, it is courage that is an Advent trait, mirroring a fearful virgin's *yes* to some unknown future and risking thereby every other possible future. Like some Isaiahan spirit reconciling calves with lion cubs and befriending lambs with wily wolves, courage enables us to say yes in the face of life about to be fractured, yes to a call that ultimately makes life whole.

It is courage that enables us to bring strength to the weak, even though we fear being weakened ourselves. It is courage that makes tough love *love*. It is courage that enables us to stand by our convictions at the expense of our own social or economic security. It is the courage of Mary that once made Advent new and still makes us new in every Advent.

> *upon arriving, the angel said to mary:*
> *"rejoice, o highly favored daughter!*
> *the lord is with you.*
> *blessed are you among women."*
> *she was deeply troubled by his words,*
> *and wondered what his greeting meant.*
> *the angel went on to say to her:*
> *"do not fear, mary.*
>
> *mary said:*
> *"i am the maidservant of the lord.*
> *let it be done to me as you say."*
>
> *luke 1:26–38*
> *immaculate conception*

4

When Someone Turns
the Question

I F WE COULD HAVE BEEN HONEST AS KIDS and dared to say aloud what I even now hesitate to put down on paper, we may have admitted then that summer vacation could be too long. For some reason or other, however, we always sensed (and still do, I suspect) that there was some unspoken code that if one was true to being a kid, one had to be *for* summer vacation — for all of it, from the June school bell to the September school bell and every breath of sweaty play in between. The truth of it is that there were times without anything to do, and that the number of those times grew in inverse proportion to the days of summer remaining. In fact, those days even had their own motto, certainly worthy of any banner: "What is there to do?" We drove our mothers crazy with that plea until, drained of suggestions, they would shout us out of the house and insist we create our own "stuff to do."

Recently I listened to a small group of high schoolers snared in the discussion of how to bring about a just and equitable distribution of resources. There is no guilt-free way out of such a discussion; we have all been there ourselves. Yet the issue needs to be raised and the question asked. The gathering concluded, as they always do, with someone asking in frustration, "Well, what can we do?" There it was. The banner may be faded and frayed, but it is the same banner passed on to larger arenas and longer parades.

Same words, different questions. Steerage through life is filled with someone changing the questions on us, and worse — never telling us until we are well into the answers. Just after we have finally begun to learn how to find "stuff to do," how to "lego" fun into our lives, the question is changed. Suddenly it becomes no longer a matter of building lives for ourselves, but rather a matter of building our lives for others. And just as when we were tykes, still no one tells us how. "Love one another," we are told. "Feed the hungry." "Forgive." Flip answers, it seems, to a task no one has ever quite been able to master, no one except the one who first taught us.

There is a sense in which those teens gathered as children that evening and went home as adults. In the space of two hours, someone changed the question and put the world on their shoulders. No longer could they only play at life. They had been given responsibility — without asking for it. The course had been marked, as it is for all of us — regardless of whether or not it is fair. Once immersed in that spirit, there is no going back to innocence, only ahead to sanctity.

It is the storytellers and the poets of our land who change the questions, I think, or rather move us from one question on to the next. It is the weavers of tales and the singers of songs, the Spielbergs and the Springsteens. Some time back there was a marvelous film entitled *Madame Sousatzka*. In a society grown stale with people lusting after love and wondering how to possess it, that film quietly rephrased the question to "How does one love without being possessive of those we love?" Suddenly, how to hold on to love seemed old, like so much dried bread. The question had been turned.

From generation to generation, from gathering to gathering, there have always been those who have asked the question and done so with fiery passion. It may have been Martin Luther King or Dorothy Day, it may have been Joan of Arc or Francis of Assisi or Elizabeth of Hungary — but before them all, there was Jesus who came first with spirit and with fire.

> *the crowd asked john,*
> *"what ought we to do?"*
> *in reply he said,*
> *"let the man with two coats*
> *give to him who has none.*
> *the man who has food should do the same."*
>
> *luke 3:10–18*
> *advent*

5

Those Who Dance in the Womb

S OME THINGS BEGIN BEFORE THEY BEGIN. Days begin with an alarm or a radio or a nudge in the ribs; they begin so often in the dark, before the suns rises. A college education begins before September, even before high school graduation. It begins at least with kindergarten and perhaps even before. A marriage begins with a date or with infatuation or with a blush, but most certainly it begins before the Mendelsohn parade. Some things — perhaps most things, begin before they begin.

Christmas begins before Advent. It begins when the local backyard swimming pool franchise replaces its displays with decorated trees. Or it begins when Halloween cards are taken from the shelves. Or it begins when someone comes home and says, "Guess what decorations I saw in the department store today." Or it begins when you hear the first carol on the radio. Or it begins when a jolly white beard in a polyester red suit drawn by twelve mechanical reindeer slips into the local department store window amid swirling autumn leaves. Or it begins whenever it begins, but most certainly it begins before Advent — in Bethlehemish fashion, "too small to be among the clans of Judah," or the clans of front-page reporting, or the clans of noteworthy excitement. Christmas begins before it begins, and it begins small, not unlike the divine and holy "yes" sounding so much like a feminine voice.

Like Christmas, what we become also begins before it begins. We live in a cacophony of stimulants — some creative, some not so, but none simply there. And the spirit-child in the womb of

22

our life dances to each. The cornucopia of wants overflowing our shopping malls, our addictions of music, muzak, and more-zak, our bifocaled saturation with television and film, our drives for gourmet sex and passions of the pallet fed until the menu becomes bizarre — all of these and more create a society of continual wants incapable of being satisfied and of needs dulled into silent oblivion.

Yesterday's newspaper wrote of how we have become self-sufficient and self-contained individuals — no longer needful of one another. We have become islands, the article went on, content to be adrift in the stream to nowhere. But it is not so. We are not whole unto ourselves. To the contrary, we have become a people incapable of being islands — whether of silence, or of creativity, or of insight, or of hope. Neither have we become a united mainland. Rather, we have become so addicted to the outside that the inside has all but died. We have become a people so stimulated that we have been hypnotized into paralysis.

What we become begins before it begins. The hollow world around us, in the end, has hollowed us. And into that void, into that emptiness, born in Marian fashion, comes the divine surprise, wombed as are we. And once more, like John the Baptist before us, we leap for joy — this time as never before. It happens when someone is kind and we notice it — nothing grandiose, nothing bombastic, just kind — simply and quietly. It echoes in our emptiness, and for an instant we catch ourselves wishing we too were so kind, so gentle. And we begin to dance.

It happens in the midst of crisis and tragedy when we have been emptied of a future. Powerless, we surrender, resigned to the lifeless present; and in that surrender we come upon a new movement of life and strength — one that sustains without any source because it is the source. And the spirit within us dances and leaps for joy.

It happens when we have been overcome by our sin — real sin, heavy sin, crushing sin, when who we were is no more. And into that nothing comes a whisper of peace, enfleshed just enough to be heard; and we are made new, not returning us to innocence but refashioning us into goodness. And our joy knows no bounds as we dance in the womb to a divine rhythm played upon our spirit.

What we become begins before it begins, in Bethlehem-ish fash-

ion, too small to be named. But that is how it is when God is born —
then and now. That is how it is for those who hear the divine song
and are willing to dance, even in the womb.

> *who am i that the mother of my lord*
> *should come to me?*
> *the moment your greeting sounded in my ears,*
> *the baby stirred in my womb for joy.*

> *luke 1:39–45*
> *advent*

6

A Human Sort of Christmas

CHRISTMAS IS NO LONGER GENTLE, it seems to me, as it shoves and pushes its way out of shopping malls, trying to find its way beneath our trees. Nor is it any longer simple, as when ornaments did not have to follow color schemes or decorator designs, and the variety of Christmas sweets was found in varying shapes and colored sugar rather than at the neighborhood cookie exchange. Strange, too, how for some these days come with dread, turning lighter hearts weary for all the tasks that garland the season. It has become more civil than religious now, I fear — at least not for a few.

On the other hand, it may be that I am just a cynic, foil-wrapped in the nostalgia of a Christmas that once lit our trees and played our radios and now does so only to our memories. In the end, I guess, we simply want the days to be special — or perhaps it is that we *need* them to be special. We work so hard to make them all the best of what it is that makes us human.

We are more generous in these days and are even trimmed with justice. We who have more than what we need grow more aware of those who have less than what they need; and we make sure they have enough — of food, of clothes, yes even of Christmas presents, when the unnecessary and squandering delight of gifts becomes a necessity. We are indeed "unscrooged"; and the preoccupation with self is set aside as so much tinsel.

We Christmas truce our wars — both personal and national — and thus give peace at least a one-day chance to shine upon our Bethlehems. We recognize, as well, that we are not as fiercely independent as we would like to think, that we cannot live without the paper boy or mail carrier or babysitter, at least not very well. And so we bless those quasi-marriages to strangers with a bit of token gold. We try to smile a bit more readily, answer our phones with a touch more warmth, sing songs with hearts a-carol, Christmas our tables with friends, and believe that even the have-to's are worth it all in the end.

Perhaps the reason we grow so tired through it all is that it takes work to be human — to be peaceful and forgiving and generous and just. To be human in such a way (is there any other?) is indeed no small task — even for God. Thus in the beginning was God's Word, and for billions of years it was with God. Then once in our history it was spoken and lived so clearly, so forcefully, that people came to see it and name it God's Word Made Flesh — Yeshua Messiah. And ever since then we have tried to live that way ourselves. For the most part, we have not succeeded in any great way. But we do work at it — at making God's Word flesh in our own lives. Some days we do it better than other days; some times it is more visible than at others; and for one season, this season, there are more of us coming closer to being human than at any other season.

> *the word became flesh*
> *and made his dwelling among us,*
> *and we have seen his glory . . .*
> *of his fullness*
> *we have had a share —*
> *love following upon love.*
>
> *john 1:1–18*
> *christmas*

7

Love Somewhere in Between

I T WAS ALMOST FIVE O'CLOCK in Milwaukee's downtown area, and all the business families were closing their doors and their windows and going home to their other families. People were going home to love, or to love lost, or to love somewhere in between. In one way or another we were all going to that one place that frames our experience of meaning.

That is, in the end, what we are all about — seeking out love, seeking out someone for whom we make a difference, someone who wants us back, someone who needs us even when we are at our least best selves. That is certainly why we give presents in this season. We want to say, "I love you;" or we want to say, "Please love me."

For some reason or other, however, all of us seem to get lost in that temple of love, trying to be about the "Father's business." We get lost in a maze of anger, dead-ending our relationships. We get lost in a jungle of possessions, forgetting how to sort "keepers" from "losers." We get lost in ourselves, forgetting to forget ourselves. Yet what is amazing is that somehow the "Father's business" does get done, in spite of all the efforts to twist it into our business.

It is not difficult for us to slip into naming the church's business as God's business — or perhaps more properly naming the institution's business as such. Maybe it is because we need to justify our preoccupations with permissions and dispensations and good order that we find ourselves insisting that somehow God not only

27

cares about it all, but even insists upon it all. And suddenly God's church has been turned into our church rather than vice versa.

For others the sacraments have become the "Father's business" — not however as invitation but as obligation, not as God's way of breaking into our lives but as our way of breaking into God's. Have-to masses, limboed baptisms, communion — wrapped first in confession, all of these we have decided God wants and needs. Odd, too, that we should have come to define a practicing Catholic as one who "goes to church." Odd that that has taken on greater significance than service to the poor or a simple lifestyle or a genuinely pro-life attitude.

What is even more amazing than how we have turned the "Father's business" into church business, however, is that God still lives in these temples. In spite of it all, the Word continues to be preached, people come to know a loving God and are able to grow in deep genuinely spiritual ways, the poor are ministered to, wisdom surfaces. People come looking, like Joseph and Mary, because someone said he was here, and they find him; they find love. *We* find love — as if we have come home from the business of life.

We do come to this temple, however we have found it to be. We come to love, or to love lost, or to love somewhere in between. And while most often it is somewhere in between, we do find it; and having found it, we keep all these things in memory, like Mary.

> *his mother said to him:*
> *"son, why have you done this to us?*
> *you see that your father and i*
> *have been searching for you in sorrow."*
> *he said to them:*
> *"why did you search for me?*
> *did you not know i had to be*
> *in my father's house?"*
> *but they did not grasp what he said to them.*
>
> *luke 2:41–52*
> *feast of the holy family*

8

Wishes at the Seam

A S THE CALENDAR TURNS so does the year until each is new. And with their turning we find ourselves reflecting on the year just past — whether it was good or not, whether marked by death or by life, what it is from the year that we will carry on into the next.

In so many ways it seems such an arbitrary marking of days, for the turn from December 31 into January 1 is no different from the one from July 25 into July 26 or from May 23 into May 24 or any other day of the year. Yet this one at the seam does draw us into a backward gaze, and then perhaps quite naturally into a forward dreaming as well, for to see the year's wounds and scars is to find oneself also longing for the healing.

And so it is that we make resolutions — or at least talk about making them. Sometimes I wonder if anyone really makes resolutions anymore — if it is a custom grown in disuse, or maybe even a conversation piece of what we all talked about but never did. On the other hand, it may be something we give up as we grow older, coming to discover that we are who we are, that seldom in life do we make radical shifts in the way we live. Perhaps that is one of the gifts of youth — believing not only that we can be more than what we are, but also believing that we will be.

Yet whether we actually make resolutions at the turn of the year or only talk of them, they are, nevertheless, there — the looking to the future and recognizing that for each of us life at least could be more than what it is. And we put that vision into words.

My suspicion, however, is that for many of us resolutions are more like wishes — like pieces of life it would be nice to have in our purse or back pocket but seldom so serious about as to pay the price. We resolve (or wish) to lose weight or save money or exercise regularly or quit smoking or pray more or watch less TV or be more patient or whatever it is our lives crave at that particular stage of unfolding.

The fact of the matter is that the resolutions or wishes are in reality symbolic of deeper hungers. Our wish to be more patient really flows from a need for peace in our lives. Our resolution to lose weight or to exercise regularly may well have its source in our longing for health, or more accurately in our longing for life and the desire to possess it. Our hope to save money reflects the security we seek, and our sense that we need to pray may upon reflection stem from our need for meaning. And on and on and on. What we wish for so often points to what our spirits long for, and what our spirits long for is ultimately God — the God who *is* peace, the God who *is* the only security possible, the God who *is* life and meaning and beauty and hope.

Curiously, we have made God in our own image and likeness rather than discovering how we have been created in God's image. We have given God arms and legs, a face and a body, and a robe of all the shortcomings of our own humanity. The truth is that we have been created in God's image, created to be peace and love and life, created in an image that hungers to be what God is. Our spirits do cry out "Abba!" — the one source who is all for which we long. The spirit of God's son has been sent into our hearts, and as a result we are heirs, daughters and sons of our God.

> *the proof... is the fact that*
> *god has sent forth into our hearts*
> *the spirit of his son*
> *which cries out "abba!"*
>
> *galatians 4: 4–7*
> *mary, mother of god*

9

A Change of Stars

W E WHO STAR-TREK OUR WAY through the deserts scattered about our lives are ever in search of the "right" star on which to hitch our dream. Yet no one seems to know which the "right" one is. And so we jump into each day faster than the day before, as if there were only one star to catch before it falls, only one gold ring to snare before it tarnishes.

It is no great secret that we are a people on the move. Our rush-hour expressways siphon people in and out of our cities often by a lure many cannot name. Airports jet us into "friendly skies" filled with our angry frowns. Even our psyches spiral their way into a frenzied vortex of oblivion. Styles change before clothes wear out, and sometimes even before we have time to wear the clothes. We spend our evenings in front of televisions flicking not only channels but frazzled nerves with machine-gun rapidity. Our need for the constant new panics at the thought of eating the same food two days in succession. Our rush-hour journey through life has indeed made the novel so ordinary that we are at a loss as to how to celebrate the new. Not only our bodies but also our spirits have become drugged with change and speed. We want it all — now — before it turns to nothing, with the fear it may already have. And so we rush even faster.

A recent newspaper article reported that science has discovered a star eighty billion light-years away — a star so far that it takes light traveling at the speed of light eighty billion years to make its way to our backyards. Such reality simply shatters not only yesterday's reality, but also any literal God or heaven or rate of spiritual

31

exchange. We feel foolish even toying with the idea that perhaps the place of heaven might then be at the ninety-billion-light-year marker; and we find ourselves wondering how our traditional piety can any longer be holy. Forced into redefining our once human-faced God and our heavenly cosmic "other home" — all by a star eighty billion light-years away — we rush into distraction.

The other day Kim told of how she and her sister were talking about whatever it is sisters talk about. In the midst of it all, her sister looked at Kim and said, "Kim, you're not going to make me think, are you?" Kim smiled as she told the story, but also with a bit of sadness. And she was right about it, you know — the sadness, I mean. We rush through our tangled lives, oblivious to the tangles, oblivious to the universe eighty billion plus light-years away, but mostly oblivious to the whispered call urging us to make an inner journey of eighty billion plus light-years as well.

The star gazers who found themselves at Bethlehem most likely came packed with all the tools of their astrological trade — with incantations and potions and charts to match the paths of stars with those of men and women. It has been suggested that the gold and frankincense and myrrh were among those "tools" — brought on a journey out among the stars only to have discovered that the real journey had all along been one within, like a personal black hole catapulting their consciousness and awareness deep within themselves. In an effort to discover the Lord of the universe among the stars, they came to understand that the only real universe was the one within, and there the Lord would always dwell.

Whatever it was that brought them to that realization left them radically new in a way that could never be old. Whatever it was moved them to surrender those tools of their original quest and to offer them — the gold and the frankincense and the myrrh — as gifts in submission before their new Lord. In the process the three itinerant astrologers became three wise men.

> rise up in splendor, jerusalem!
> your light has come,
> the glory of the lord shines upon you.
> raise your eyes and look about.
>
> isaiah 60:1–6
> epiphany

10

Choosing Up Sides

THE HORROR of having to "choose up sides" for a game was never the possibility of someone else being chosen first; the real horror was always the probability of being chosen last. In fact, the reality of being chosen last was that you were not really chosen at all because at that point in the sorting process the inevitable was obvious to both sides. When you were last, you quietly drifted over to "your" side while field positions were being assigned.

There are, of course, other choices made for us (whether by the gang or by life) — many of them falling into the "hafta" category. "Why do I always hafta be the one to take out the garbage?" (back in the days before garbage disposals) or "Why do I always hafta take my little brother along?" or "Why do I hafta be the one to set an example?" Always it was "because I told you so, and you should do these things anyway."

So it was and always will be — more of life's "choosing up sides" are levelled without any input or consent from the chosen. We are chosen by life to be the eldest (or the youngest, as the curse may be), chosen to be male or female, cute or plain, adopted or not, healthy or sickly, lovable or obnoxious, and on and on and on. There is little in life, it seems, over which we have any "choosing power." Perhaps that is why so much is made of who gets to decide which TV program will be watched or what we will have for supper or what color to paint the bathroom. Most of the time *life* chooses *us; we* are not able to choose *life.* And much of the time what life seems to choose for us, we would rather life hadn't.

There are those rare moments, however, when we do feel

blessed — when we do feel life has "clicked" (if only briefly). Just once we happen to be the ninth caller to the radio station and receive two tickets to the baseball game or the sports show or *Bimbo and the Waltzing Rhinoceroses*. Just once we do receive a promotion at our job or we have our turn at Andy Warhol's "fifteen-minutes-of-fame" or the doctor says, "You're lucky. It's not cancer." Just once we are not chosen last.

Of all the lotteries into which life has dropped our name, perhaps the greatest prize is falling in love. Love simply happens to us, without explanation or reason. It is pure gift, undeserved and unearned. We do not choose love; love chooses us, whether we are in search of it or not. It seeks us out in a gathering of a hundred people or explodes with force in the quiet privacy of our room. It discovers us buried in the busiest portion of the day or bobs alongside us adrift in our daydreaming. On a mountain top or in a hovel, in the midst of success or lumbering with failure, when we are serious or when we are silly, it is love that chooses us, and not vice versa. Yet as much as it is a blessing to be chosen by love, it is also being chosen to enter death — the painful flip of a two-sided coin of gold.

There is often tedium, and more often pain, as parents nurture a new-born spirit through adolescence and into adulthood. Some would call it love and others would name it death, but the label matters little, for there is only one nurturing reality. Bruises need gentle healing, whether it be a sapling humbled by an icy storm or an ego bowed by a stormy life. Then no one asks if we want to be the healer. Then we are simply chosen, as Jesus was, because we are there. And we cringe a bit — wondering whether we have been chosen by love or by death. The answer of course, as always, is "yes." Strangely we never quite get used to either of them. Whenever we are chosen, whether by love or by death, it is always as if it were for the first time. Perhaps a part of that is because they are one and the same.

In the end, being chosen by love is the only prize. There is no other, because there is no other game except the game of life; and in that game there is no other love except that which also calls us into death. It is God's Spirit bursting forth upon all of us at one time or another, except that this time when we choose up sides, the marvel is that somehow each of us finds ourselves chosen first.

here is my servant whom i uphold,
my chosen one with whom i am pleased
upon whom i have put my spirit.

isaiah 42:1–4, 6–7
baptism of the lord

Part Two

TIME IN BETWEEN

Part Two

TIME IN BETWEEN

11

Water into Wine into Life

THE GROOM'S GREAT UNCLE was there among the wedding guests — not so terribly unusual in itself despite the fact that at the age of ninety-two he was probably the oldest guest at the wedding. What was unusual was that that same great uncle was himself just married earlier that year, and married for the first time. Amazing, and so marvelous — someone marrying for the first time at the age of ninety-two. For him, no doubt, life had not run out of wine. For him there must have been much joy and much hope still to taste and with which to celebrate. And I sat there in quiet awe of him.

Life is not always so for everyone. Life does run out of wine — perhaps for all of us at one time or another. We look at our relationships and find ourselves saying, "There is no more wine." It may be a friendship of five months or a marriage of five years or a marriage of twenty-five years — but for some the wine does run out. For some of us it is our jobs when they lose their challenge, or the dream tarnishes. Or it may be when one day the foreman gathers everyone to announce the closing of the plant. In a moment all of the jobs have turned to vinegar; there is no more wine. Still for others it is when retirement suffocates the future, and all of that which once gave meaning is choked and dies.

The very same may be for a community, when life seems to have no more wine. It is the hopelessness of living among the jobless urban poor or the depression of fallow fields among the rural poor. It is the loss of life-blood for a town or city when its one manufacturing plant shuts its doors both on the labor force as well as on the force for hope. It is so for the illegal aliens, and those who are gay, and those without education, and anyone else without hope — anyone else whom the rest of society calls "Desolate" or "Forsaken."

There are those times, however — if I might turn the page — when hope is reborn, when we feel "Espoused" not only by life but by our God, when the ordinary turns extraordinary and the water becomes wine. Such are moments worthy of celebration as at a marriage feast, for they are moments of joy and delight when God breaks into our lives. It is the phone call offering a new job after we have gathered checks for months of emptiness. Then the ordinary becomes extraordinary. It is the monotony of growing old turned to new wine by a visit and a hug from a grown child or a grandchild. It is falling in love when one has given up waiting for love. It is the quiet silence at the end of a day that screamed its way onto our calendar. It is someone who listens, finally, when no one else would or did. It is conceiving a child after years of barren waiting. Such are the times, and many others as well, when we are caught off balance and trip into God unwittingly, saved from drudgery and redeemed to live life enriched, when water is turned into wine.

For all of us, I suspect, life's banquet has been served up in such ways — at times without wine and at times renewed by a wine whose source no one seems to know. But it is the wine that makes the difference — the hope that brings a quiet, deep-filled joy to life, that reveals God's presence, and its absence that leaves life empty and thirsting for meaning. It is the wine that turns life not only into a banquet but into the celebration of our marriage to our God. It is then that we realize as never before that we and our God are indeed one, that we are made new in our God, that the time *has* come — the time when our God looks at us and says, "My Delight."

no more shall men call you "forsaken,"
or your land "desolate,"
but you shall be called "my delight,"
and your land "espoused."
for the lord delights in you.

isaiah 62:1-5

at a certain point the wine ran out,
and jesus' mother told him,
"they have no more wine."

john 2:1-12

12

A Lifetime of Forever

C AN ANYONE SAY FOREVER? was the title of the book — naming an unknown quest and an undiscovered hunger in many an American, for deep down where our spirit lives all of us long for something that is not passing. We find ourselves living in a society saturated with dreams and possibilities, but also in a society short on commitment, short on forever. It is not, however, only the permanence of our relationships that our lifestyles call into question, but all other forms of our commitments as well — our professions, our hobbies and playful distractions, our neighborhoods, indeed all of our hopes and dreams. Having been promised that we could "have it all," we find ourselves strangely empty-handed and empty-hearted, wondering how it could be that gold dissolves.

A recent newspaper article observed that we have few great artists in our society — few so talented with brush or with pen, few so skilled in dance or in drama, that without hesitation we would recognize them as great artists. And the reason, posited the observer, is that there are so few willing to commit themselves to life-long pursuits. We have come to realize, too clearly, that by choosing to open one door, we thereby seal all the others, forever — and this too many of us are not willing to do.

It is easy when we are young to choose a dream, to choose an overriding purpose for our lives, that which will give meaning to all we do. The menu of dreams seems gourmet then, and the choices unlimited. And if the taste does not satisfy, there is much time to order another.

But there comes a time when we realize that the choosing was the easiest and the simplest. Then we come face to face with the fact that not everyone shares our dreams, or that we do not possess enough energy for more than one dream, or that the one we chose (if we are faithful to it) will take a lifetime of effort. That is when commitment takes place or when it does not — not at the choosing, but at the point of crisis. And that may occur on the same day as the choosing, or on the next day, or in the next year.

At some point those who choose a dream, whether it be that of marriage and family, whether it be one of service to the community or neighborhood, whether it be to achieve wealth or fame, to build an empire or conquer someone else's — at some point they will be faced with the question of cost and of commitment. It is every dream's second choice to which some say yes and some say no.

It was so for Jesus. In the temple, with the neighborhood gathered about him, he named his vision "to bring glad tidings to the poor, to proclaim liberty to captives." It was on the hilltop, however, at the cliff when both dreamer and dream were about to be hurled over, that the vision faced commitment and with it the ability to walk on out through the adversity. It is at this point, in the flat lands of a marriage or in the stale bread lines of service, that love then becomes patient and kind, not self-seeking or prone to anger. It is at this point that love prevails, or it is not love.

Can anyone say forever? Of course. *Does* anyone say forever? Of course, many do, but never simply once. It takes place again and again and again, whenever someone faces the monotony of a marriage or the tedium of raising a family and chooses to make it last for one more day — just as they did the day before. It takes place whenever someone chooses to continue to live in a changing neighborhood in spite of the turmoil fringed with risk. It takes place whenever people continue to struggle with human limitations — their own or others', whenever they dance to music no one else can hear. And they do so not because there are no alternatives but because they realize there is no life without their dying — for them or for anyone. They do so because there is no other world than the fractured one in that they live, no other world than this one which is in the process of being redeemed, all the while teetering on the cliff.

before i formed you in the womb i knew you,
before you were born i dedicated you,
a prophet to the nations i appointed you.
they will fight against you,
but not prevail over you,
for I am with you to deliver you.

jeremiah 1:4–5, 17–19

13

When the Owl Calls

SOME HAVE MORE AND OTHERS LESS, but all of us come to find stretch marks on our lives — those scars left over from the growing pains of life. All of us have had to work at making life liveable. We are pulled and shoved, despite our prayers and bargain pleading, into what would seem to be the crippled alleys of life; and by some unfair and arbitrary lottery we seem to be barred from the sun-filled avenues of joy and ease — at least as we would choose to know them. We are jobless in spite of the ladder of success we set up, or bonded into a marriage less than the dream, or journeying through lives perpetually scattered with potholes. And so all of us, some more and some less, but all of us, have been stretched by life, unwillingly ushered into one or another void.

If the truth would be known, however, more of the fullness is to be found in the void than is found in the cornucopia. What has promised to bring life, has not — a lesson taught to each generation as it assembles the jig-saw puzzle of wisdom reassembled by every succeeding generation.

It is the yuppie community of believers that has been most recently disillusioned by the creed that promised fulfillment and life. A decade ago they subscribed to the articles of economic faith. They attended the prescribed universities and became the CPAs of our society; they bought the properly addressed condo and drove a BMW; they dressed in three-piece suits and joined the best of clubs. Having achieved it all, they wondered how it could be that at the age of thirty their overflowing lives could be

45

so empty. What they sought, they had achieved, and then realized they had been deceived. Like Pepsi or Coke in the desert, it does not satisfy.

One of life's contradictions is that by journeying into that which is empty, there we find what fulfills; by entering what is void of all we seek, there in some miraculous fashion we come upon an overflowing draught of what it seemed could not have been there. It is like Peter who is invited to cast his nets into the very same barren waters he had just fished and found nothing, only to haul them in, straining with the sea's harvest. Having been called into a void he never would have chosen, he finds a fruitfulness he never would have imagined. It is the movement of God in human life — having nothing to do with catching the fish of the sea, obviously, but having everything to do with gathering in the spirits of men and women.

Much (some would say all) of the wisdom we have come to know in life has been the gift of pain and struggle that stretched us to the edge. None of us would ever have chosen that journey through pain, nor would any of us ever have wished it upon another. Yet I suspect that for all of us the insight and wisdom to which we came, there at the edge of our lives, is something none of us would ever surrender.

A friend who is a recovering alcoholic speaks openly about living with the disease of alcoholism and how it has influenced her life. She frequently makes reference to the recovery process and all that it has taught her. Alcoholism is a terrible disease, she will firmly assert, yet she also insists she would never surrender the insight and life-skills brought through recovery — a very mixed blessing, indeed. For her, alcohol was survival and life and meaning without which all would be lost. Yet it was only without it, by entering into the consequent void, that she and every other recovering alcoholic could find authentic survival and life and meaning. It was by casting her net into a seemingly barren world that she came to find an overabundance of what she always had sought, and in the process found the only Lord of Life.

The invitation to death and to its emptiness comes in many forms, at many times, and to all peoples. Among the Native Americans of our land there is a legend about the approach of death — if you hear the owl call your name, know that you have heard the call to die. If, then, you should hear the owl, answer clear and strong and without fear, "Here I am. Send me."

> *simon answered jesus,*
> *"master, we have been hard at it*
> *all night long and have caught nothing;*
> *but if you say so, i will lower the nets."*
> *upon doing this*
> *they caught such a great number of fish*
> *that their nets were at the breaking point.*
>
> *luke 5:1–11*

Part Three

A TIME BEYOND—
of Lent & Seeking

14

A Desert Named Purple

L ENT COMES IN MANY COLORS, but mostly in purple — winter purple, heavy and serious. Purple is the color of sorrow and of conversion — or maybe, for us believers, *post*-conversion conversion, when we are called to change and we really do not know what we are supposed to change to or change from, when it seems that our lives are really okay, or at least not so bad. And then suddenly it snows purple, blanketing us with would-be repentance.

Perhaps that is why we do not like Lent, or at least why there are many who do not — because it deceives us into looking at corners of our lives we would rather leave unnoticed. Lent is as sneaky as our sin and just as subversive. It slips in under the guise of doing penance — like giving up desserts or saying an extra prayer each day or not swearing; and then it hooks us into remembering (or maybe realizing for the first time) that world hunger demands more from us than our just desserts or that prayer is not a generous "extra" or that swearing may very well be a question of who will be allowed to be God. It is then that Lent begins to rub off on us and turn us not only purple but black-and-blue from trying to fight our way out of God.

If I Were a Horse is a child's fantasy story about Jenny who daydreams about being a horse and then changes her mind as she realizes no one may recognize her. But it is more than fantasy, or rather more than child fantasy; it is the human fantasy of sin, which tries to redefine the world in our terms, like believing we can become a horse just by our deciding it. It is our lying that attempts to redefine truth in terms of what we would wish life to be rather than in terms of naming life as it really it. It is the alienation with which we choose to live, attempting to redefine life on our terms by granting *de facto* existence to some and denying it to others by pretending they do not exist. It is our addictions that redefine the source of life and meaning to be not in God but in us and in our wants. Lent brings us face to face with who we are — which is not a horse (real or otherwise) but, by God's design, a son or daughter of that God, or else no one may recognize who we really are.

Lent does come in many colors, often in our own fantasy colors, but mostly it comes in purple, calling us to a post-conversion conversion, calling us to recommit ourselves to life as it has been created rather than attempting to recreate it in our own image. Little wonder that we back away from Lent, then, for to enter into it is to embrace the world as it is and there begin the process of a transformation that takes place in us.

Such are the temptations of Jesus that mirror ours — or ours that mirror his. It is the same movement of spirits belonging to different worlds — attempting to name the real bread that sustains (which is really a question of what makes for better bread — God, or the "stuff" with which we build our own little worlds?). It is struggling to recognize which kingdom is real and which is illusory (which is really what Jesus was always talking about anyway — is the real out there? or is the real within?). It is standing on the pinnacles of our own temples, thinking we can get God to adapt to our world rather than our adapting to God's (which is really our blasphemous attempt to convert God). We and Jesus are spirit-brothers and sisters journeying through the same desert turned purple for the struggle.

Somewhere, then, in the course of each Lent, all of us either give up or give in. We either give up because dying gets to be messy and painful, putting into violent disarray our neat and ordered lives. Or we give in to this purple monster by the name of Lent who tempts us with the craziest of promises into believing that holiness is possible and that life is sown in seeds of death. Then we do pass up desserts, not because we think God may be interested in desserts, not because we need to lose weight, but because we need to reenter a world in which we do not satisfy every craving — and desserts are only a symbol of that reentry. Then we do pray, not to convert God to our way of thinking, not to change the world as we would have it, not to foster any contentment, but simply because it finds a home for our wandering heart. And having done so, purple takes on a royal warmth.

> *jesus, full of the holy spirit,*
> *returned from the jordan*
> *and was led into the desert*
> *for forty days,*
> *where he was tempted.*
>
> *luke 4:1–13*
> *lent*

15

Hardly Anyone Wants to Die

NOBODY WANTS TO DIE ANYMORE. I mean, nobody wants to unravel a part of their life for someone else. I may be simply nostalgic for the activist 1960s (though they certainly had their own shadow side), but those were days of Peace Corps dreams and VISTA possibilities when people packed up their energy, put their own futures in storage, and, with all the naïveté that youth could muster, sauntered into someone else's yard to build a better sandbox. It may have been a bit presumptuous, but certainly well intentioned. And though the new and better worlds tarnished just as quickly, at least their hearts were sterling. Now, it seems, no one wants to die anymore, at least almost no one.

Something shines through when people choose to do some dying, and it is not a glossy ego. Dying transfigures us and makes us transparent — though sin and selfishness do so just as readily. But choosing to die gives it all a different hue — almost that of divinity. There is a difference, even if the words are not there to say it right.

Perhaps the reason no one wants to die has something to do with the society in which we live. It forces us to want it all and feel deprived if we do not. It is America, after all, we tend to think. We should be able to live next door (or not live next door) to whomever we wish. We should be able to send our children to any school of our choosing. We should have a right to life the way we want it — to growth without pain, wisdom without growing old, health without ever a day of illness. The consequence, of course, is a world without God, for it is always in our dying that we are transfigured.

It is always the dying that reveals to others the human face of God.

There is a poem by John Updike entitled "Fever." It is about coming to faith in the midst of deep illness — which is a kind of dying of its own.

> I have brought back a good message from the land of 102°:
> God exists.
> I had seriously doubted it before;
> but the bedposts spoke of it with upmost confidence,
> the threads in my blanket took it for granted,
> the tree outside the window dismissed all complaints,
> and I have not slept so justly for years.
> It is hard, now, to convey
> how emblematically appearances sat
> upon the membranes of my consciousness;
> but it is a truth long known,
> that some secrets are hidden from health.*

There comes a time, then, when we realize we must not only be willing to die but also we must choose to die because the situation in which we live cries out for dying in order to be transformed. We choose to remain in a changing neighborhood simply because someone must; and if it is not us, then who? We listen to a "bore" day after day with the realization that that bit of love may be the other person's one thread to meaning and survival. We commit ourselves to long-term service because some devils can only be cast out by great love, unrelenting and unceasing. Such dyings clothe life in dazzling brilliance — an entirely new kind of glory.

A friend died some time back. He was one of those individuals who, when driving down the street, would always stop to allow some other driver to slip in line from out of a driveway or parking lot. He did it regularly. And whenever anyone would ask, "Why?" (and there were many who did), he would always say, "You've got to, or it'll be a jungle out there." It is the times we choose to die, small as they may be, that transfigure us and allow the face of God

---

*Copyright © 1960 by John Updike. Reprinted from *Telephone Poles and Other Poems* by John Updike, by permission of Alfred A. Knopf, Inc.

to shine through, for if we do not, the world in which we live will
indeed be a jungle of dark and hollow faces.

> *jesus' face changed in appearance*
> *and his clothes became dazzlingly white.*
> *suddenly two men were talking with him —*
> *moses and elijah.*
> *they appeared in glory*
> *and spoke of his passage*
> *which he was about to fulfil*
> *in jerusalem.*
>
> *luke 9:28–35*
> *lent*

16

Scorched by Burning Bushes

L IKE THE TRIANGULAR SCORCH MARKS burned by the tip of the laundry iron upon the back of our careless arms, life leaves its own brands upon us all. And they do not disappear quickly, if ever — not the burns from the laundry iron nor the events burned upon our memories, not those in our personal lives nor those in the life of our nation. Like photographic negatives able to be read by the untrained eye only in reverse, so too are the events of our lives more clearly understood in reverse, with 20/20 hindsight. Nevertheless, however or whenever we read them, they do not go away but remain etched upon our consciousness, branded by life.

Those who survived the atomic bomb in Hiroshima and Nagasaki described with horror the happenings surrounding those days. Among their memories they recalled how the brilliance of the light burned silhouettes into concrete and stone, so intense was the flash which in an instant changed not only the landscape of their cities but also the landscape of the world's psyche. Ever since, the world "turned nuclear" is a different world because its people are a different people, and they are different because of what they remember.

America has not been able to forget the assassinations of John F. Kennedy and Martin Luther King, events which compelled us to admit we had lost our innocence. Watergate stained us with an ugly mistrust of those who lead us — a finish that needed to be stripped to bare wood before we could be re-finished. The conflict in Vietnam created as much division and anger and resentment at home as it did in Asia, and it is still not forgotten. Our national psyche, which once saw itself as righting every wrong and over-coming every injustice, has been forced to recognize in itself the very traits it sought to uproot from others.

Such events serve as bonfires marking a nation's path decade-by-decade through each century. And those fires, those psychic markers, continue to burn for each generation until each becomes the last generation to tell the tale, until one day only the stories are remembered with no one to remember the happenings. And should a decade pass without such an event (as in the 1950s and perhaps the 1980s), then we feel as though we have drifted through our history without a mooring by which to tell our tale. The very same events that torch our history also light our history.

So it is with our personal lives as well — the birth or perhaps death of a sibling, a family move to another neighborhood, the suicide of someone we loved, a grandparent's moving into our home, divorce by our parents, finding a best friend, life-threatening illness, a first love. All of them become the events by which we mark and measure our lives in terms of before and after. They are more often tragedies than celebrations of success, strangely, and thus are also remembered as turnstiles of growth. But each of them sears itself upon our consciousness, shaping and forming not only our lives, but our very selves as well.

Should we begin to read our lives in reverse, sorting and inter-preting as we mentally make our way through the maze, a person of faith quite naturally begins to ask what God was saying through it all. We realize, then, that those markers, those bonfires, were the burning bushes before which we came face to face with our God. We come to see, more clearly as more of life is lived, that life is indeed holy ground — all of it, with God woven throughout all of history, woven in and out of the fabric of all that is and of all that takes place, indeed even the very fabric itself. It is no longer a matter of God being present to life. God *is* life, a constant I AM.

As much as I may regret how I have ironed my shirts, scorch marks and all, I must necessarily wear them that way or go shirtless and bare-backed. So must I come to know my God, not without struggle and often in pain — yet *there* face to face, or else *no where*. The bushes continue to burn.

an angel of the lord appeared to moses
in fire flaming out of a bush.
moses decided, "i must go over
to look at this remarkable sight,
and see why the bush is not burned."

exodus 3:1–8, 13–15
lent

17

Goings and Comings Home

HAVENSWOOD IS JUST THAT — a wooded haven from the city, wedged among those neighborhoods beginning to show wear. It has become a nature preserve now, but it was not always so, nor was it intended to happen. Its hundred plus acres were swampland once, then filled in for a city prison when adolescent Milwaukee did not need the space it now does. After the prison was outlived, the land was given a new face by the military, and Havenswood became a missile site in the 1950s. The land was cored, and the round hollows were lined with concrete — silos meant to store not life but rather death.

After the Nike missile program was dismantled, the land was redressed by the city with hiking paths and prairie growth. A nature center grew up at one end, and stands of birches at the other. A hollow was reformed, and the swamp pond from earlier days returned. The fields harvest butterflies now, and hawks and owls sew the sky to the earth as they wing their way between the two. It is almost as if the land has been reconciled with its earlier innocence.

In a back corner of Havenswood the now empty missile silos have been left in memory of history. Each holds only a cache of darkness now, their lids sealed by the weight of flower planters built upon them. In the summertime the covering grass grows green, ground critters nest beneath shrubs, and the overflowing blossoms play a melody of beauty for gazing eyes. The land of Havenswood has returned home.

The journey home, then, is not always made along paths and roadways, but often times along the instincts of our hearts as well.

The return to where we once lived, the return to what we once were, is made in many ways. In fact, given the opportunity, all life does heal; all life does return home. Polluted skies wash themselves clean. Broken hearts as well as limbs do mend. Those taken advantage of learn to trust once more. With rest, the farmed soil is renewed, just as Havenswood forewent its violent heritage. It should not, then, be surprising that, given a full-featured lifetime, sinners return home as well, with home waiting in patience as though it knew the outcome all along.

The urge to return home from our journey into sin is one of the mysterious movements in our spirit — almost as if a homing device were planted within us. Some would name it human nature, others conscience or guilt, still others the stirring of God's spirit. But the name (as in most of life) matters little, only the resting place. Having caroused our way through adolescence, we do come back to the wisdom sown in childhood. We squander our present as well as our dreams over possessions, and in the end surrender them all for the sake of love — just as we learned love before everything else. The resting place does matter — of course it does.

I suspect real conversion comes, however, after we have tasted many tables, slept in many beds, and wandered through many yards only to realize we were continually the stranger. Many would challenge and even insist that sinners repent and convert. More often I find myself wondering, however, if it is not *conversion* that finds *us* — finds us lost and disoriented, desperate for home if only someone will point the way. Like the younger son in Jesus' story of the Prodigal Father, life often exhausts alternatives, leaving the only path as the wisest path. It is then that we come home, surprised that what we find was waiting all along. The story of Jesus, we then discover, is not so much meant to teach us what we must do (such as "to return home from our sin") but rather it is meant to describe the journey we have just completed. Only the home-body recognizes the tale as his or hers.

Like Havenswood, life does return home, whether we are conscious of the process or not. We need only sufficient time to recognize the journey. And, like the father's two sons in Jesus' story, the return of one portion of our life so often marks the departure of another.

> *coming to his senses at last, he said:*
> *"how many hired hands at my father's place*
> *have more than enough to eat,*
> *while here i am starving!*
> *i will break away and return to my father."*
> *... with that he set off for his father's house.*

> *luke 15:1–3, 11–32*
> *lent*

18

The Hardest Thing We Do

MAYBE IT IS TRUE. Maybe forgiving is the most difficult thing we have to do — worse than having to stand in line at the supermarket or waiting in a doctor's office, worse than having to hang up our clothes or clean the house or do our homework or go to the dentist, worse than growing old or not being old enough. Forgiving is not fun. It is difficult, sometimes very much so, because it means letting go of our world and being willing to live in another world — one that has the bits and pieces of a lot of other lives.

Most of us are not very good at forgiving; or maybe it is that we do not want to be very good at it. We hang on to sin, ours and everybody else's. We hang on to ours because we like our sin, and we hang on to everybody else's because we think their sin makes ours look less twisted.

As unforgiving as we can be, so can our society — though why that should be a surprise I am not sure, since we are the "stuff" of our own world. When the state of Florida eventually executed Ted Bundy in January of 1989, people cheered the arrival of the hearse and threw "Bundy parties." Those who are divorced live lives tattooed with a scarlet "D." AIDS continues to be gleefully touted as a deserved "divine affliction." The prejudices of our own culture we have reshaped into the sins of others, and we refuse to let them pass — "blacks do not want to work," "welfare mothers are promiscuous," "women are weak." Forgiving does not come without difficulty.

When Sharon's two boys — one five and the other almost four — spark her frustration and her anger by their constant friction, she sits the two of them at their play table, but without any play. And she insists that they stay there until the two can laugh together. Having laughed away their anger, she reasons, they will have also laughed away the memory of their pain. They will have forgiven one another, and, having done so, they will be able to get on with the rest of their lives, or at least with the next ten minutes.

Forgiving, however, is not forgetting. There is a difference, for though we may be able to decide upon the former, we are never able to choose the latter. Strange and peculiar folk that we are, we tend to nurture our hurts — the very things we curse. We like to taste them, like savoring good wine again and again though never having noticed that the wine has become vinegar.

At some point, however, we need to let go of those hurts. It is then that we forgive, and also then that forgetting begins, for the ability to forget is simply a generous gift flowing from our willingness to accept and forgive. Like Sharon's two sons, upon freeing the one who has hurt us, we are set free ourselves.

Without mercy the sinner is frozen, as if the ice age has returned as some frigid Vesuvius. Like a child's doll cast in perpetual infancy, without mercy we have no future. Mercy recognizes the power of the human spirit and believes in that spirit. It trusts us with the future. To forgive, then, is an act of faith — not only in human persons (that they can be more than what they have been), but also in the Spirit of God that animates each of us (indeed, Jesus kept insisting that the reign of God does dwell within us). It may very well be that the refusal to forgive is that unforgivable sin about which the gospels speak, for to refuse forgiveness is to deny that Spirit that "makes all things new."

In the past, too often justice and mercy have been forced to a face off — as in the classic confrontation between the woman caught in adultery and those who brought her before Jesus. Then justice becomes victimized by mercy and mercy by justice. It is in Jesus, of course, that justice and mercy become one, when he insists that the most just stance is to assure the woman that God's mercy is as available to her as it is to her accusers. Suddenly the rock-strewn desert is barren of stones, and the few that remain are too heavy for throwing.

> *remember not the events of the past,*
> *the things of long ago consider not;*
> *see, i am doing something new!*
> *now it springs forth,*
> *do you not perceive it?*
>
> *isaiah 43:16–21*
> *lent*

19

Of Dreamers and Dreams, the Gathering and the Emptying

W HY IS IT that the very things we chase after elude us, and not just once in a while but almost all the time? It is not only the "biggies" of life that so often seem to escape our grasp — the job we stretch to find, the falling in love that never seems mutual, the financial security that is in perpetual bankruptcy. With these we have a sense that there are only a limited number of such "biggies," and we have to wait our turn. Much as we pursue these, we also understand that life has its own rhythm beyond the control of our personal whims. However, it is also the little satisfactions that seldom seem to come our way, especially when we need them — the ten minutes of quiet peace somewhere (anywhere) during a day played at full volume, a teenager who says just once, "Gee, Mom, that was a good dinner," just one week between December and March when everyone in the family is healthy and no one has a cold. Even the little perks seem to be rationed on a schedule.

Calvin & Hobbes (everybody's ego and alter ego disguised as a comic strip) finds Calvin griping, "I'm not having enough fun right now." And when Hobbes wonders, "You're not?" Calvin takes the opportunity to vent his frustration. "I'm just having a *little* fun. I should be having *lots* of fun. It's Sunday," he laments. "I've just got a few precious hours of freedom left before I have to go to school tomorrow. Between now and bedtime, I have to squeeze all the fun possible out of every minute! I don't want to waste a second of liberty! Each moment I should be able to say, 'I'm having the time of my life right now!' But here I am, and I'm *not* having the time of my life! Valuable minutes are disappearing forever, even as we speak! We've got to have more fun! C'mon!" As the two race off toward that day's finish line, Hobbes says, "I didn't realize fun was so much work." And of course Calvin's wisdom is beyond even Calvin, "Sure! When you're *serious* about having fun, it's not much fun at all!" Unfortunately, that which we so energetically seek, we seldom ever find — yet strangely, except when we surrender the quest. It may all simply be another one of Murphy's Laws, along with "When you drop a piece of buttered bread, it always lands butter-side down" and "Find an empty parking space, and it's sure to be on the other side of the street."

Life not only has a wisdom of its own; it also has a spirit of its own, often contrary to the best laid plans of mice and everybody else. It is a spirit that brings us to fulfillment, but at times accomplishing that in spite of our own best efforts. Some would even suggest it to be the Spirit of God that seems to empty us of all our doings, if for no other reason than that we then might be filled by God's doings.

We tend to spend the early years of our lives gathering dreams of one kind or another. We dream about what we will be when we grow up, of how we will be famous or rich or powerful. We fantasize our "dream home" and the perfect marriage and family to live in it. We dream of having many friends and of making a name for ourselves — of how life will someday be. Then somewhere in the middle of our lives something happens, and a switch begins to take place. Having spent half of a lifetime gathering dreams, we begin to find ourselves letting go of them one by one. We look at our bank account and realize we will never be wealthy, and we allow that dream to slip away. We look at our family and discover that it is not the family or marriage we had always dreamt it would be — not that we do not love our family, nor that it is not good, but it is simply different from the dream we had. Our home is simple, and our clothes not glamorous; and we gaze into the mirror and upon our face with its wrinkles and our head with its gray hairs (or perhaps no hairs) — and it is one more dream we set aside. We open the door of the medicine cabinet in our bathroom and find bottles of pills — all testimony to our frailty. We climb stairs a bit more slowly, play tennis with a bit less enthusiasm, and go to bed at night a bit more early. In the quiet of our heart, one more

dream — the dream of youth — is set aside. Those with whom we
have shared life and love die, and we are forced to let go of them —
but barely. Finally, in the end, having let go in the second half of our
lives all the dreams we had gathered during the first half, we stand
clinging to one last dream (though none of us would dare admit
it). Nevertheless, in the end we are finally forced to surrender even
that one final dream — that we can live forever. And then, having
been emptied of all that we have possessed, then in the image of
Jesus we are filled with life and resurrection, for (in the words of
Mother Teresa) "even God cannot fill what is already full."

> *your attitude must be christ's:*
> *though he was in the form of god*
> *he did not deem equality with god*
> *something to be grasped at.*
> *rather, he emptied himself*
> *and took the form of a slave . . .*
> *obediently accepting even death,*
> *death on a cross!*
> *because of this,*
> *god highly exalted him.*
>
> *philippians 2:6–11*
> *palm sunday*

Part Four

BEYOND TIME—
of Resurrection & Life

20

Leftovers among the Tulips

W E HAVE BEEN "PARADOXED" BY LIFE and find that most of it is
double-notched with contradictions. Life is simply not the
way we thought it would be, but always downside up and outside
in. When we were kids we could hardly wait to grow up. Then we
would never have to do all the dumb things kids have to do. We
wouldn't have to do our homework or wash the dishes or take care
of little brothers. We would be able to stay up as late as we'd want
and not have to eat vegetables or take baths. Being grown up *had*
to be better than being a kid. Then, wham-o! The calendar flipped
by in years instead of months, and we find ourselves as adults —
adults who wished we could be children once more, adults who
have discovered that being a grown-up has not shed the problems
we had in childhood. For some reason or other, what we wore in
childhood we find ourselves still wearing today.

When we bumped into one another at the jelly bean counter, it
had probably been two or three Easters since John and I had seen
each other. We tossed the usual how-are-ya's back and forth a time
or two, and then I asked him about his family. "Just fine," he said,
and then smiled a bit sheepishly. "You know Amy and Jack are both
graduating this year — one from junior college and the other from
high school." (I had forgotten how quickly kids grow when you
turn your head.) "Well, they keep asking me what they should do
with their lives. Crazy kids! They don't know I haven't figured out
what to do with my own yet, and here they are asking me what
they should do with theirs." John laughed when he said that —
knowing it to be not all true, yet maybe more true than false.

As kids we had always imagined that when we became adults, childhood would be cast aside, or at least preserved between the pages of our book of memories to be rediscovered in later nostalgia. It seemed then that adults always knew what life was about, what the right thing was to say, what wisdom called forth in each situation. Now, here was John finding the leftovers of childhood's uncertainly still scattered about his own life. What we wore once in childhood, we find ourselves still wearing today.

We once thought grown-ups were always confident and secure, only to recognize now on the canvas of our adult lives the brush marks of our childhood shyness. The procrastination that nurtured postponing grade school homework continues to linger in today's job jars. Indeed, we continue to trip over the cast-off wrappings of an earlier life that we thought had died in adolescence. And such is not to say that we are still children, but only to admit that the new life of adulthood is born through a process of dying not yet complete.

Our paradoxed lives are so much like the days of Easter themselves, especially when the calendar's rhythm births the season prematurely. Easter is supposed to be puddles of daffodils and tulips, with tie-dyed eggs dipped in rainbows and little-girl smiles ruffled in pink. It is supposed to be new life spilling over like the resurrection it is meant to mirror — except that too often it is not that, especially when it comes in March or early April, still scarred by winter. In such days crocuses spear their way through the last crusty snow and turn their purplish-white faces toward the coming Easter — the season's first life amid the leftover wrappings of lingering death. And the robins return, but always too soon — before the springtime thaw can serve up the still frozen banquet. Finally, of course, a breath of Genesis-like spirit, and spongy fields are resettled with cracking bats and screaming baseball and kids with soakers — but always before the wind can dry up the puddles of leftover winter. It is springtime at last, and no one can miss it, except that all the wrappings of an older season are still scattered about. That is how it is with birth; that is how it is with life; that is also how it is with faith.

Even believers live a curious mixture of yesterday and today — of what we were and what we are, regrets and hope, sin and grace, death and resurrection. Sophie had lived and died a good person, her life draped with the simple trappings of faith from another era. Rosaries and litanies hung from the corners of her life; Lenten penance was sewn into the fabric of every year; morning prayers and evening prayers bracketed each day; what she had, she shared generously, for life did not need to be extravagant. Sophie's goodness mirrored her faith; yet when she came to die, she did it with an anxious fear that unsettled and confused her. How could a person of faith also fear death, she had often wondered.

Yet Sophie was no different from us all. We profess to follow the Lord Jesus, yet drag along our sin. We trust that God will make all things new, yet hoard our past for some apocalyptic day of rain. We give over our lives to God's presence, yet sigh and groan with the rest of creation. None of which is to deny the resurrection, but only to recognize the wrappings still lying in the tombs where death once lay. Even believers must live with the paradox of life, with the tension of being human. Having died with Christ, our new life continues to remain hidden.

after all, you have died!
your life is hidden now with christ in god.
when christ our life appears,
then you shall appear with him in glory.

colossians 3:1-4

peter got up and ran to the tomb.
he stooped down but could see nothing
but the wrappings.
so he went away full of amazement.

luke 24:1-12
resurrection day

21

The Adolescence of Believing

HAVING SPENT SCATTERED TIME laughing and crying with teenagers in their molting years, watching them be transformed from children into adults while cocooned in adolescence, it seems to me that something radical happens to them during Christmas vacation in their junior year of high school. Prior to that year's Christmas, it is always difficult (nay, impossible) to engage them in a serious, significant reflection upon their lives or their faith or their meaning. Not only is there no interest or inclination, there is not even an understanding of the question. And then they return from being immersed in twinkling lights and garland and ribbon, and it is as though in this particular year of their lives they themselves become the Word enfleshed. Do not misunderstand; it is not that they return as enthusiastic evangelizers of the world, but they do return able and even willing to enter a serious discussion of their own faith for more than one minute — and that has, at least for me, about the same impact as if they returned as enthusiastic evangelizers. It happens every year, with every group, and is one of the mysteries of faith, lacking explanation but nevertheless real, and somewhere in significance between the Trinity and transubstantiation.

Yet I must confess that being a believer is much like being an adolescent your whole life long — which is perhaps why many adolescents are not enthusiastic believers, for only one such journey at a time is about as much as any one person can endure. Faith, too, comes in awkward clumps and spurts that stretch us till we hurt, and then we are not even sure whether it is growth or gangling confusion. And so the believer lives with feeling lost, as if he were from some other world, as if she did not belong, for suddenly what is real no longer fits the definitions. Faith is being forced to live in two worlds — like the adolescent who must pay the full adult price to "catch a flick" yet not be old enough to drive a car, who must find a job and so begin to earn her keep and yet account for where she went and what she did. Adolescence is not fair, and neither is faith. Like puberty, faith just happens; and like love, it sometimes doesn't.

We try out gods, it seems, the way we try out lovers — or fantasize about them when we are young and revel in a giddy playground of discovery. Then both gods and lovers etch memories upon our lives and evermore the temptation, as well, to make those memories the measure of future loves and future gods.

Such is the stuff of which nostalgia is made, which sires both infatuation as well as religious enthusiasm. The premature creeds to which we nod and give assent, then, come forth from godly memories instead of memories of God. In those adolescent days of faith

> we believe in Christmas cribs and curling incense,
> in hardwood-kneeling pain and wimpled discipline,
> in acolyte bells which consecrate our Lord
> and turn him into bread and wine,
> and vigil lights which hold our God in bondage
> to our wishes.

It is, of course, more pleasing to believe in a Jesus both dimpled and swaddled and in a Spirit confirmed by oil instead of by struggle.

At some point, however, the nostalgia of religious memories must be sacrificed upon some altar — as if it were the life demanded in offering, not by God but by faith. It is never the past in which we believe, though Thomas tried (in vain) and sought Good Friday's relic wounds. Such is the stuff of which tradition is shaped, but hardly faith. For faith is Spirit present, always believing without seeing simply because believing is a different way of seeing. Then we believe because someone has risked to roll back the stone of fear that has kept her life entombed. Then we believe because someone, wrapped in revenge, has been unwrapped and has stepped forth in forgiveness. Then we believe because we have known men and women crucified upon oppression who continue to live and do so in freedom. Like Thomas, we would have expected the familiar Jesus, wounds and all. Like Thomas, once we see with faith, we have no need of Good Friday's wounds for we have seen the risen Lord enfleshed in our brothers and sisters, and because we have placed ourselves in *their* wounds, we have believed.

> *it happened that one of the twelve,*
> *thomas (the name means "twin"),*
> *was absent when jesus came.*
> *the other disciples kept telling him:*
> *"we have seen the lord!"*
> *his answer was, "i'll never believe it*
> *without probing the nail-prints in his hands,*
> *without putting my finger in the nail-marks*
> *and my hand into his side."*

> *john 20:19–31*
> *resurrection time*

22

A Rorschach Sort of Life

IT IS THE TALE OF GOLDEN HANDCUFFS. A man and woman marry and sculpt their future with artistic care — a stylized family, a *Better Homes and Gardens* home and garden, membership in a country club to taste a bit of the country, some travel in order to learn and good schools in order to travel, in time a second home to vary the first, and all securely blueprinted upon the foundation of the "right" profession. Somewhere along the way, however, somewhere midway through the dream, they find that life has changed their taste in art. What they had begun to sculpt is not the piece with which they want to live. The stress is high and the routine is routine. Socializing has grown shallow, and the challenge of business has become bitter. But it is too late to redesign the blueprint, they come to realize, or too costly, or too damning. They find that one or the other (or both) enjoy the amenities. Downscale housing would be embarrassing. To reshuffle the social deck would confuse the game, to say nothing of the children. And so there is no choice but to continue building a castle that increasingly becomes a prison — "golden handcuffs."

There is, of course, a blueprint out of the malaise just as there was one in — but it must be crafted with all the deliberateness and planning and sculpting as was the first. The journey out is the journey in. Like some Rorschach ink blot pressed between the pages of life, endings do mirror beginnings — except in reverse, which is how mirrors work anyway. Sunsets reflect the sunrise, though opposite in pattern. Springtime sows the fields

with seeds that then die and sprout and grow and blossom and
bear fruit and shrivel and then return to seed, only to await another springtime. And of course we humans are no different. We
are born helpless and dependent, only to find our lives returning there after the years pass — giving over in just the same
way all that we had once gathered one by one. Though the
thought may well be accused of presumption, we are tempted to
wonder if the Creator could not have been more creative in her
plan.

A long time ago I remember a doctor's reply having the same
Rorschach vision of life when a patient asked how long it would
take to get well. "How long did it take you to get sick?" the doctor
wanted to know — which is the same as saying that endings mirror beginnings, which is to say that the way out of the golden
handcuffs is the reversal of choices that cuffed life in the first
place, which is of course no different than Peter and Jesus face
to face in the resurrection. On the night before Jesus' death, Peter
had done a quick, three-step shuffle of denial outside the San-
hedrin. Now, a week or so later, Peter finds himself face to face
with "Do you love me?" — not once but rather a trilogy of undoing. The original journey out of love and into sin set the pattern
for the final journey out of that sin and into forgiveness. Life is
filled with ink blots, usually black and murky and always double faced — a fact we fail to recognize or, perhaps, *prefer* not to
recognize (which was, by the way, Peter's initial response to the
shoreline stranger who wondered if they had caught any fish).
Life has a way of masking what is real, and thus we live in illusion until the resurrection unmasks the mask and the illusion
fades.

So life is an assortment of journeys in and out — the former usually chosen by us and the latter chosen for us. We tan-
gle our lives with selfishness or greed or sin until life becomes
unbearable, forcing us to unravel the snarl. We hide in the silence that entombs a marriage until its echo is so deafening
that we are forced to speak and thus slowly breathe life into
a would-be corpse. Denial drags us into addiction till we are
set free by another's courage to confront and drag us back out.
We have sorted our colors into neat, segregated boxes of living, until the violence we bred forces a dismantling — except
that the anger dismantles more slowly. Then, like the disciple

Jesus loved crying out to Peter, we recognize the voice, "It is the Lord!"

> *as a young man*
> *you fastened your belt*
> *and went about as you pleased;*
> *but when you are older*
> *you will stretch out your hands,*
> *and another will tie you fast*
> *and carry you off against your will.*
>
> *john 21:1–19*
> *resurrection time*

23

Told Even by Dandelions

LIFE IS ALIVE WITH MORE THAN LIFE. There is a rhythm afoot among all that is, a wisdom beyond its years — not simply some master Houdini creating illusions with his cosmic sleight-of-hand, not some trickster of the universe who knows all the hiding places and teases us into playing hide-and-go-seek among creation. No — life is alive, and the rhythm is more than just life.

On the ever-illusive calendar of Wisconsin seasons, springtime comes with the flip of a coin — sometimes early, like an eager suitor arriving at the front door ahead of his watch, and sometimes late, stumbling in and tripping with confusion as though apologizing for the alarm that failed to ring. Yet whenever spring does arrive in Wisconsin — early or late — the dandelions bloom full-force and unfailingly on Mother's Day weekend, the second of May's four. Life *is* alive with more than life, responding to a call we may not hear.

There is, as well, a never-ending battle waged between Lake Michigan and her shoreline tenants claiming ownership. Like some Don Quixote challenging the ever constant windmills, those who claim to own the rim of the lake strive to keep the lake from re-claiming the cliffs and sandy beaches — yet always with futile energy. Disintegrated footings from earlier sea walls and re-enforced concrete now twisted and mangled scatter the beaches as skeletal remains in memory to the effort. In curious defiance, the lake almost seems to have a mind of its own.

Strangely enough (or perhaps not so strangely), our own lives are played upon that same instrument. Too often, *most* often, the dreams we pattern and the hopes we plan seldom bear their fruit. The best of that for which we strive seldom comes to be. On the other hand, as if by some law of contradiction, that which we have come to cherish and hold as most dear is usually that which we never even imagined as possible, and yet it came about, almost in spite of our best efforts in another direction.

Science has pushed the Big Bang that created our universe back to between fifteen and twenty billion years ago — a time beyond our imagining. The 2000 years of Christ-time in relation to those twenty billion years, however, is the equivalent to two seconds in relation to a year. Suddenly we begin to understand how Christianity is but the beginning of a new era, and our own lives are but blipped breaths in the unfolding. We stand amazed at the immensity and marvel at the becoming of something we are not even sure we understand — yet it is simply one more piece of creation in process, guided by a spirit that embraces us as well, a spirit that embraces us with love never to be lost.

Whether it be blooming dandelions or shoreline erosion or the happenstances of our own life, there does seem to be some sort of spirit woven through all that is, drawing everything in some magnetic-like fashion toward culmination. Neither a random unfolding nor a predetermined manipulation, life is most certainly alive with more than life. It may very well be the same energy that a parent brings to guiding a son or daughter through childhood and adolescence. It is neither abandon nor control but a wisdom in between that we have come to name as love. Small wonder, then, that St. John's mystic meanderings into God should have come to the same conclusion.

Life is alive with more than life, drawing all unfailingly into its presence. Moment is built upon moment, and one step gives direction to the next. Universes blossom, and springtimes explode with color bubbling up from the earth as if some volcano of life could be held back no more. Goodness comes to the surface in spite of sin, and our lives bear fruit without us even knowing how. Such is the journey, one without end, on which we are led into life. Indeed, all is coming to be.

my sheep hear my voice.
i know them,
and they follow me.
my father is greater than all,
in what he has given me,
and there is no snatching out of his hand.

john 10:27–30
resurrection time

24

In Quest of a Better Light Bulb

W HEN GARRISON KEILLOR created Lake Wobegon, he spun a place where all the women are strong, all the men are good-looking, and all the children are above average. The possibility that life could be whole and new captured us then and continues to capture us now, and we wait for its coming. "See, I make all things new!" said the One who sat on the throne, and we wonder why he is late in showing his face.

We wake up each morning with an unconscious hope that more than the sun might be new, longing for the time when the rain does not fall on our picnics and leaves do not fall from our trees in the autumn, when no one argues and everyone agrees — whether it be about the best flavor for ice cream or the one most qualified to be president. We secretly wish for the days when everyone gets an "A" in every subject, when children never have to be punished, when those who love always grow old gracefully and die together, and when lawns sprout without dandelions, tires never go flat, and the paint never peels off our houses. If God is in fact making all things new, why is it not happening in our world? Why is this world the way it is?

I suspect, however, that God may well think this is not such a bad world — given the possible alternatives. And besides, what God is making new is not our grassy yards or dim light bulbs or quasi-stylish fashions. What God is making new is our ability to forgive (having been rusted tight with revenge) and our spirit to serve (having been served upon for too long) and our generosity (having befriended some crotchety greed along life's way). What God is making new is us. The world out there is fine just the way it is; it is the world within that, unfortunately, needs to be transformed.

It is a process going on in us all — whether we are aware of it or not, whether we agree to it or not — and we enter into that new world, into that kingdom of unrippled peace and inner joy, through human struggle. It takes place not as if there were some divine barter exchanging happiness for suffering, not as if God were some sadistic scrooge hoarding human pain, but rather simply by our entering into our human weakness and there confronting ourselves with honesty and with courage.

It happens to the high school jock as well as the middle-aged businessman caught in the vice-grip of a need to win, a need fed by a fear of losing, versus a very human need to be freed from that fear and realizing the only way is *through* losing. It happens to the mother whose world is her children, discovering then that her children have grown into *their* next world, leaving her without a world. It happens to the addictive person who comes face to face with the reality that she has been seeking a solution outside herself for problems existing inside herself, and that the only solution is to admit those insides. It happens when someone finally realizes he must forgive and will most probably spend the rest of his life forgiving those same hurts, and that such forgiveness is the only way out of self-destruction. It is in such moments and many others as well that we are made new — not by choice but by agreeing to live with who we are and discovering that in doing so we become more than who we were or ever thought we could be.

We will all undoubtedly continue to seek a new and better world. It is a hunger sewn into the warp and woof of our lives. And so we cannot do other than believe that somewhere we will find a Lake Woe-be-gone where all the women are strong, all the men are good-looking, and all the children are above average. The surprise, however, will be to realize that instead we have been given a world where we have learned to love one another.

they gave their disciples reassurances,
and encouraged them to persevere in the faith
with this instruction:
"we must undergo many trials
if we are to enter into the reign of god."

acts 14:21–27

i, john, saw new heavens and a new earth.
the former heavens and the former earth
had passed away.
the one who sat on the throne said to me,
"see, i make all things new!"

revelation 21:1–5
resurrection time

25

All Those Who Ride Silver

"WHO WAS THAT MASKED MAN?" ask the town folk as the savior rides off into the sunset wearing a gunbelt full of silver bullets. They never know, of course, yet neither does it ever matter, for they have been saved from evil and have been restored their town or their future or their lives or whatever else was being threatened. What is significant, however, is that the hero rides off, leaving the home folk with their home. Had he stayed, the "home" would have always been his for he was the force that brought salvation. It would have belonged to him for he had freed it from evil — only then he would not have been a savior but a conqueror. And so he gives the "home" back and in doing so gives back much more. In doing so, he gives back to the townsfolk their freedom, their worth, their dream, their world, and in payment he is given everlasting glory.

They say we never really grow up until both of our parents have died. And it is true, I suspect, for then we can no longer go home, we can no longer go back to security. Having lost the home that once cradled us (no matter what the age or where we lived), what we are given then is the present along with the task of building there a new home. But it is the dying that empowers us — strange as that may seem — and *saves* us from being eternally imprisoned in the past. It is their departure that brings the process of salvation into our lives — whether it be the departure of our parents or the masked man or the Lord Jesus.

The very fact that that process can become a burden speaks worlds about who it is who is doing the building. It is the work of our lives, and we wonder why it must always be us — why *we* always must be the one who must say, "I'm sorry," why *we* must always be the one who plans the evening out or writes the Christmas cards or calls your mother or spends time with the children or absorbs the pain of a dying parent or even a dying child. Yet such is the business of building worlds — of healing both spirits and bodies, of creating joy, of designing bridges into the hearts of others — all because the unmasked Messiah rode off on a cloud of silver into the right hand of God and thus gave back to us our lives.

> *"you will receive power*
> *when the holy spirit comes down upon you."*
> *no sooner had he said this*
> *than he was lifted up before their eyes*
> *in a cloud which took him from their sight.*

> acts 1:1–11
> ascension

26

Brothers, Sisters, Cousins, Ants

L IKE SEEDLINGS cracking through the earthen crust left by winter, people poke their heads out doorways and windows as if to test the springtime with their noses. Too much too soon and they might be nipped. But when the litmus comes back positive, windows spring open as if on cue, and door frames become the Arc de Triomphe through which the victors, home from doing battle with winter, pass in parade. There is more to this season than warmth, or color dribbled and dabbled, or shattering the shackles of cabin fever. There is a flow at the heart of it all that makes everything new, when in the silence one can hear the stones hum and the trees gurgle, when even the human spirit responds in kind, singing four-part harmony with earth and wind and fire. As if some Franciscan genealogy was rediscovered each year, we come to realize anew that all creation shares a common kindred.

In its own time such a realization finds each of us. Go on a picnic and spread the blanket, place the food and wait for the ants. Those who have just begun the journey into life will kill the ants to save the food. Those who have known that journey and have come to value life will lift the ants from the blanket and place them back upon the grass. Those who have come to treasure all of life as sacred, however, will feed the ants. There is a harmony that urges us to recognize a common kindred to all that is, even among the ants. We are all one with one another, and springtime is the herald of such news.

We need to listen to the calls our bodies and our psyches make upon our lives, for there is a truth they whisper to us. Just as we thirst when our bodies are in need of fluid, just as we crave salt or meat when bodily supplies are depleted, just as our spirits long to hold and to love when we are lonely, so we need to pay heed to the hunger that longs to make all things one. It may very well be one of those human rhythms that, if ignored, will bring death just as surely as will all the others when they are ignored.

That hunger to reconcile and bring our lives into common harmony shows itself again and again. It is recognized in the midst of divorce, always a two-edged sword severing with every move that deep need for wholeness in our lives. Divorce is painful precisely because it shreds our lives and our loves and our dreams. If the union was ever a marriage, divorce can never simply be a casual parting, for it threatens within us the very possibility of wholeness.

Curiously, as well, we find ourselves rooting for the underdog as if a victory will make life whole and bring equality to some of life's imbalances — whether it be on the field of battling sports or in the world of business intrigue or among the triangles of love. We have a need that life be fair — at times even questioning whether a God who does not seem fair can possibly be God.

Just as keenly we know the need to mend our relationships. Anger scattered throughout our days remains scattered throughout our nights, reminding us each time that "I'm sorry!" does more to welcome the muse of sleep than *Sominex* or late-night reading. Families cast in the silence of anger remain rigid and lifeless. Working in an environment without peace is less work and more war. The need to apologize and to forgive rises as well from deep within our beings, an urge unable to be suppressed without destroying our very selves.

There is something within the very texture of life that seeks to make all things one. It blossoms in the spring, but also in the human heart — sometimes as spring fever and sometimes as infatuation. And not to give it heed is to know that somehow we shall all be less, for we also know that such is what we have all been called to be from the very beginning.

jesus looked up to heaven and said:
"i have given them the glory you gave me
that they may be one, as we are one —
i living in them, you living in me —
that their unity may be complete."

john 17:20–26
resurrection time

Part Five

SPIRITED TIME—
of Fifty Days & More

27

A Very Common Good

SOMEONE NEEDS TO CARE FOR THE COMMON GOOD; and while that person need not be common, that person must be good. It could be the role of the government, though it is tempting to suspect that lobbyists have polluted the goodness there, making favors all too common. As a nation we have slowly drifted from democracy to capitalism and in the process have surrendered the common good to the monotheistic worship of individual rights. It may very well be, then, that the Spirit (and the community in which it lives) is the last champion of the common good.

I rummaged through the calendars my memory hadn't tossed, searching for events when the common good had been preserved, and I smiled to myself at the many moments of Spirit the diaries held, though also knowing full well not everyone would agree. But that is okay; there is no other way to name the Spirit.

I lived through the Vietnam era — much easier than most, I sheepishly admit. It was the conscientious objectors, however, who brought me to my senses, more than anyone else; they were some of those with Spirit who called for the common good in those Nixon days. And Jimmy Carter, who tried to build a cobblestone path of human rights through the meadowland of world nations, he tried, and sometimes failed; but the very fact that I still remember must say the Spirit lingered there and lingers still. And Mikhail Gorbachev (a contemporary Cyrus, who ultimately became an instrument of the Lord, allowing the captive Hebrews to return to their homeland after exile in Babylon?) — are Gorbachev's dismantlings of one world for another of the Spirit? Yet that is too much of the now to know with certainty — or perhaps not.

I am grateful, too, for Federal Judge Barbara Crabb, who upheld the Chippewa treaty rights to spear fish in northern Wisconsin in the spring of 1989. She brought some wisdom (though perhaps also some fuel) to the shoreline protests aflame with anger. She insisted that justice could not be compromised for the sake of calm (whatever the prejudice), and she was right — though more of the Spirit will yet be needed to resolve the issue for the common good.

And the church (the real one, not the authoritative one), which struggles with the role of women and who should be ordained and economic responsibility and academic freedom and local leadership and making sense out of that which doesn't and loving the poor when few do and being a cry in the wilderness when most do not even recognize that we live in a wilderness — all of this is why I love the church, and sometimes (in my weaker and angrier moments) the only part I love. But that is Spirit and wisdom now, I think, defending the common good.

And parents who refuse to allow their children to play in mud puddles of selfishness and instead insist that they be children who learn to share — they too are the ones who instill a reverence and an awe for the common good. That too must be the work of the Spirit spoken with Pentecost tongues understood in any language.

All of this is of course with the knowledge of hindsight that is always much easier than plotting a course for the Spirit through today's whirlwind. What the present needs is wisdom — the ability to sort the blue jig-saw pieces of sky from those of water, all the while fully aware that the puzzle picture may not even have any water. Wisdom is the discerning process. It binds the common good to this day's reality and loosens the hold of human selfishness. It is Spirit breathed into life, thereby dismantling the towers of human babbling and enabling us to understand (perhaps for the first time) the voices of brothers and sisters.

> *there are different gifts but the same spirit;*
> *there are different ministries but the same lord.*
> *to each person the manifestation of the spirit*
> *is given for the common good.*
>
> *1 corinthians 12:3–7, 12–13*
> *pentecost*

28

The Verb *God*

MOST OF US tend to be collectors of one kind or another, though some more so than others. Some collect string until the entire house is entangled in it, or plastic bags stuffed with plastic bags stuffed with plastic bags — just in case we ever need one — or a workshop filled with odds and ends of mechanical leftovers to repair whatever piece of life wears out. But all of us collect memories, and the older we get the more ready we are to pull out the scrapbook.

We remember our first car. (Mine was a blue and white 1958 Ford station wagon owned by my brother and me.) We remember the house where we grew up. (I did my early growing in an upstairs flat above my grandparents — 1711 Erie Avenue, Sheboygan, Wisconsin). I remember, too, the chestnut tree in the front yard and the neighbor's dog, Chippy. Yet I suspect that when we stop to think about it, most of our remembering is about events rather than about objects, and that even the objects are remembered because of the events surrounding them. (I remember Chippy, the big golden labrador, because once when I was four years old he jumped up and grabbed a baloney sandwich I was eating and knocked me down in the process. And I remember the chestnut tree because of the chestnuts I collected and played with on the living room floor with my cars and trucks.) The fact is, it is events that shape our lives much more than objects, the dynamic more than the static. We remember graduating from high school and falling in love and our first job (as well as the second and third and fourth) and the death of our parents and the vacations we took and the hurts we bore and the bones we broke and the embarrassments we endured.

A while back those of us who gathered together that day were a varied and mixed assortment, a tossed salad of friendships. Somewhere along the way someone asked (as often happens) to what time of our life we would like to return, given the possibility — and the answers were just as scattered. I find the late twenties and the early thirties most exciting, a fission of new insights and new worlds. But not everyone agreed. Some found their heart in the field of adolescence sprouting with a panorama of relationships. Others longed for their twenties when dreams had not yet run out of energy. And still others treasured mid-life when both wisdom and energy combined to build rainbows. In all of us, there is a *time when*, a becoming that brands us with belonging and owned by a spirit bigger than any of us.

"What if God is a verb instead of a noun?" was the question someone else asked. "What kind of happening would God be?" We laughed when someone said, "A beer party." We laughed because it was funny — until we stopped laughing. Then we realized she was right. God could be a beer party. (There is more joy there than there is in many a corner of reality.) On into the night we served up image after image — all skewered on our imagination. Picking springtime, catching our first fish, gathering fallen stars, making love, a wild roller coaster ride, floating away in a lighter-than-air balloon, daydreaming. And after each one we would all agree. "Yes! Yes!" we'd say. "Good one," quietly wishing we had thought of it ourselves. Strange that I should remember those definitions of God better than that of the Baltimore Catechism — or maybe not so strange.

If we are who we are because of what we experience more than because of what we own, if it is the events of our lives that make us more human (or sometimes less), perhaps we do come closer to what we mean by "God" with a verb rather than with a noun. Perhaps God is a happening in whose image and likeness we are being created — except that that all sounds rather silly. But then again, maybe not.

jesus said to his disciples:
i have much more to tell you,
but you cannot bear it now.
when he comes, however,
being the spirit of truth
he will guide you to all truth.

john 16:12–15
trinity sunday

29

Ever Enough

"I'VE HAD JUST ABOUT ENOUGH FROM YOU TWO," were my mother's words cascading upon us with measured regularity as my brother and I grew not only up but also troublesome. What it was she had enough of she never said, yet somehow John and I always knew. What she had enough of was our fighting or our name calling or our laziness or our procrastination. What she had enough of was us at our worst. What she seldom had enough of was peace and quiet and cooperation from the two of us — though it always seemed a bit confusing as to just how much "enough" would have been enough.

When Carl stopped by the other day, I had not seen him in twenty-five years. His history came to be a mixture of marriage and divorce and marriage-once-more, seasoned perhaps with a bit more than the usual pain and a bit less of the good times. He explained how, during the reissued single time sandwiched between the slices of marriage, he had joined a support group for divorced men. Their overriding need, he came to realize, was not that marriage had to be a continual Fourth of July of exploding color cascading into every day, but that it had to be enough, and that sometimes one lone sparkler met that need. Marriage did not have to be one continual captivating conversation. It did not have to be sex every night. It did not have to be a relationship of fascinating interest in one another's profession. But there did need to be enough — however much that came to mean for each person. And the reasons their marriages failed, Carl came to believe, was that whatever enough came to mean was no longer found.

The story of those divorced men is really everyone's tale. All of us need enough. We don't need jazzling jewels or watches wallowing in gold to make Valentine's Day special. A gentle "I love you" or a card of thoughtfulness may very well be enough. When a clattering shrill brings alarm both to our morning and to our mind, we do not need to be able to jump out of bed and dash the one hundred; it is enough to be able to greet the day without stiffness and in good health. Nor are most of us in need of adoring fans draped over our lives in abundance; one friend, good and faithful, can well be all we need. The truth is that most often a little is quite enough. One dandelion in the middle of an endless field of misplaced dreary springtime, one "A" sprouting on a report card of averages, one child's hug in a day kissed by assorted deaths, one sliver of quiet peace when all else clamors for attention is usually sufficient to "make our day." Such are the moments when we find ourselves spontaneously grateful, when we come to discover that life has been broken open and we have been fed by the food of the gods.

Now mind you, I do not want to suggest that once we have tasted that divine bread, that then we are satisfied with no more hungers to plague our comings and goings. That is not the point at all. If anything, it is quite the opposite. Once we have tasted "I love you," once we have been nourished by the silent peal of peace in a discombobulated day, we long for more — and sometimes desperately. But what is *enough* about it is that it has satisfied our need to know that it is possible and even realizable that our hungers, our deepest longings, are not simply wishful thinking, but that they are the hints of all of that with which we will be satisfied one day in the kingdom.

So it is that all of us come to life with little more than five crusty loaves and the humiliating catch of an unsuccessful day's fishing. And it never even occurs to us to think it possible to feed a lifetime, let alone someone else's as well as ours. Yet it is only when we give it over to whomever does the feeding that we find that there was enough there all along — and we never even knew it.

taking the five loaves and the two fishes . . .
jesus gave them to his disciples
for distribution to the crowd.
they all ate until they had enough.
what they had left, over and above,
filled twelve baskets.

luke 9:11–17
body and blood of christ

Part Six

TIME IN BETWEEN

30

Life in the Shadows

L IKE DUSK, we humans are strange mixtures of darkness and light, sifted together until the two are one blend, incapable of being sorted one from the other. We are both, yet neither. We can be most generous, as is the nighttime sky with stars, and then, as if with the flip of a coin, hoard the stars in a sack of cloud. We can be both forgiving as well as vengeful, gentle and also intolerant, patient as well as rigid — all in one and the same spirit. And if it is confusing to others, it is even more so to us who must live with our unpredictable selves. Yes, we are so much like the dusk, blind and incapable of revealing reality from shadow.

The news this week reported the local tale of three women who plotted an axe murder for the past six months and then executed it with curdling violence as two of them sprung from behind a shower curtain on a male visitor to their apartment while chanting "redrum, redrum, redrum" (which is "murder" spelled backward), all because one of the women believed herself to be the mother of Jack the Ripper in a former life. Too bizarre to be real yet too real to be *only* bizarre, we find ourselves wondering what we have become. How is it that a society such as ours spins such horrors into life. Like a chain only as strong as its weakest link, are we only as sane as our weakest member? We are both darkness and light, Darth Vader and Luke Skywalker, sin and grace.

If society is bivalent, it is only because we ourselves are. The shadow side of our lives continues to shade our reality. Violence, or at least the rising edge of violence, comes to the fore in our life and we wonder from whence. Addictions plague our own sanity. Strange and violent thoughts slip into the maze of our consciousness and past the defenses with which we assure ourselves of normalcy. We are secretly conscious that somewhere along the way all of us could have easily chosen to become our least best selves. If we are frightened by what our society is becoming, it may very well be that what frightens us is the mirrored reflection of our individual selves.

Perhaps what is most frightening is that we stand before it all quite helpless, like so many snowflakes before a warming sun. We have conquered blizzards and frontiers; we have patted the man-in-the moon on the head and sat with him to toast the galaxies; we have built computers that mimic the human brain and then tease us into mental dueling; we have stretched the universe and shrunk our world. And yet we stand helpless, unable to turn prisons of punishment for the human body into hospices of transformation for the human spirit. We profess to live in a democracy and yet find ourselves forced to exist under the tyranny of a drugged society. Teenage pregnancies tear apart the lives of our youth, and the lack of motivation decays so many futures. We weep, for Al Capp was right: "We have met the enemy and they are us." In the dusk of the setting sun, all that is real lies hidden in the shadows.

We do indeed feel like foreigners standing in the presence of our God, strangers in a land of opportunity. Like the Roman centurion whose house was in need of healing, we cry out to the Lord: "I am not worthy that you should come under my roof!" — and so the healing begins, but only when we have admitted the need. That is the only place it can begin. Never as long as we pretend we are not sick. Never as long as we try to explain it away. Never as long as we struggle to rationalize why we shouldn't feel the way we do. Never as long as we believe we can bring about all healing by ourselves. Never as long as we push it down and under and out of the way and into the shadows. That is where it becomes the very shadow we fear — darker than before.

We need not be ashamed of the shadows with which we live — except that we are and probably always will be. Yet it is into the shadows that the Lord comes, for the light is bright enough and can stand on its own. It is because of our shadows that we come to

know the healing touch of our God. And so it is only by entering
the shadow that we find it to be not darkness, but simply less of
the light.

> *a centurion had a servant he held in high regard,*
> *who was at that moment*
> *sick to the point of death . . .*
> *when jesus was only a short distance*
> *from the house,*
> *the centurion sent friends to tell him:*
> *"sir, do not trouble yourself,*
> *for i am not worthy to have you enter my house."*
>
> *luke 7:1–10*

31

Touched into Summer

S UMMER SEEMED YOUNGER WHEN WE WERE YOUNG, and now we wonder if it could be that we grew older together — summer and us. Summer was more fun then, perhaps because life was more fun, and there was more of life during summer then than there is now — or does it only seems so? Then summer was swimming and crabbing down at the river and band concerts at the park and building forts in trees and riding your bike all day long and having to come home only to eat, sleep, and maybe when it rained. Now it seems we have to work at catching summer lest it slip through our lives like a hardball grounder through our glove in the field behind our house. Grown-up summers are less fun than kid summers.

Yet each year summer does come back to life and life does come back to summer. What was winter-dead is raised up and given back to us as if we were all citizens of Nain weeping for the one who made us all widows. Now as if by some cosmic touch the funeral procession into death becomes a parade of life into celebration. And we become giddy with excitement and silly children who revel in play — not only believing that with summer we have been made new, but also believing that in the process we have shed all the scars of last summer that made us old.

There is the temptation to believe that a second chance at life not only absolves the sins of the first chance but also erases the very inclinations that marched us into that sin in the first place. It is a psychic delusion teasing us into thinking that a second chance is the gift of the kingdom already fulfilled. Yet the reality is that whenever anyone raises us from our hopelessness and gives back to us a future, whenever anyone halts our death march and touches us with life, we are the same person then as we were before. Having been forgiven we nevertheless continue to live with the same snarl of human limitations — making us wonder why we ever had to promise never to do it again, which is not to deny grace, but only to recognize it as both human as well as divine. In other words, like the son of the widow from Nain, whenever we come back from the dead, we come back to the same world in which we died, with all the same people who were irritating or encouraging or frustrating or kind or boring.

Now all of this is not to suggest that we never change. We do. Except that we change slowly (most of the time), over the course of a lifetime. Ask someone if, given the opportunity to live life over, they would live it differently. Nine times out of ten that person says, "Sure! But I probably wouldn't. I'd probably make the same choices I did the first time." That is us, isn't it? Wouldn't we all like Prince Charming or Princess Lovely to come and kiss us awake to a new and happy life ever after? Yet, life among us frog-faces continues on as usual.

Instead it is the Lord who comes into our quiet, peaceful, unruffled death and raises us up and gives us back to our mother (who may very well have been also irritating or encouraging or frustrating or kind or boring). When we are brought back from the death of "no marriage," it is usually to a tangled marriage, which may just be more painful to unravel than the "no marriage" would have been to endure. When we come back from "having lost our faith" (if "to lose our faith" were ever possible), it is back to a churched faith whose preachers are just as boring as when we left, whose parishioners are just as sinful or gossiping or indifferent, whose spirituality is just as archaic or pietistic. Whenever we come back to whatever it is we left, we and it are most probably little different from when we left.

What does all of this have to do with summer? Not a great deal really — except that all of us find new energy whenever we come out of a tomb, whether it be winter's tomb or life's. And since for the most part there is a connectedness between the past and the present, between B.D. and A.D. (between before death and after death), it may well be that death is how we are renewed, ush-

ered into that moment when we are touched and given back to the
marvel of building life once more.

> *jesus stepped forward and touched the litter;*
> *at this the bearers halted.*
> *he said, "young man, i bid you get up."*
> *the dead man sat up and began to speak.*
> *then jesus gave him back to his mother.*
>
> *luke 7:11–17*

32

Americana Mercy

L IFE COMES WITH ALL SORTS OF ACCESSORIES — some frivolous and some not, some given and some seemingly earned. Good times that may or may not roll; health surviving buffets as well as being brittle; clothes that protect or Givenchy to keep power; simple homes as well as castles built in the shadows of one another; success and fame in ponds both little and big. For some the bumper-sticker philosophy that espouses that "the one who dies with the most toys wins" becomes the epitaph for life, while for others life itself is glory enough. Life *is* issued with a catalogue of accessories, and not all of them are the same.

If Americana style suggests we can buy moods and images and futures, if the catalogues from which we order life purport to list love and friendship and happiness and prestige and all else our fantasies daydream, then forgiveness becomes simply one more stock item on the inventory of available commodities. We seem to believe we can indeed buy forgiveness, while in other instances we also seem to believe we can sell it — either, for the price of someone's willingness to suffer enough.

In the film *The Mission*, Francisco kills his brother in a moment of accidental rage and then begins to drag his remorse with him through every field of life. Finally, in an effort to make life bearable, he attempts to exchange the burden of remorse for the burden of a net of heavy armor — the tools of his mercenary lifestyle. Perhaps, his reasoning suggests, the pain of physical suffering can somehow compensate for the pain of the evil brought upon his brother by his own sword. Much to his dismay, however, he is eventually forced not only to abandon his effort to equalize life (as well as the evil) but he is forced also to accept forgiveness and to accept it without cost.

Is that not so often the instance? On the one hand we seek to repay by means of our own suffering those we have injured — if we suffer enough, perhaps they will forgive us. Yet on other occasions we seek pain from the one who injured us in payment for our own pain. "If you hurt enough to balance the ledger," we seem to say, "I will forgive you." Love to the point of pain is the cost of forgiveness — all clearly described in the catalogue of life's accessories. Except that it isn't so.

If such *were* possible — to exact a pound of pain in payment for a pound of pain, then not only could we keep life equitable (which is a much easier way to live, in effect beholden to no one and once more free to make choices independent of consequences), but also we could live believing life is reversible or at least capable of having happy endings spliced onto the conclusion of sad ending tales (which is another way of not having to accept responsibility for our choices and our actions). Though we are hesitant to admit it, it would be much easier to pay the price than to be forgiven and yet forced to remember our sin. The reality is, however, that forgiveness can neither be bought nor sold.

If sin is a double-edged sword reeking destruction upon both sinner and victim, the experience of being sinned against is also a double-edged sword of pain — experiencing the evil inflicted as well as realizing that one must release the hurt and the desire for revenge, or else be destroyed once more by the very revenge we clutch. It is no easy matter to surrender the pain — whether that be the pain that we as sinner seek to offer in exchange for forgiveness, or whether that be the pain that we as victim clutch to in hope of extracting an equal amount from the sinner. Life is not fair; it comes in double doses. Such is the tragedy of sin.

If there is any prior love required of forgiveness, it is not so much love in the sinner, then, as it is love in the victim, the one sinned against. It is such love offered in the garb of forgiveness that can transform the sinner, enabling that sinner to respond then in love to others. It is not the sinner's love that brings about forgiveness from the victim but it is the victim's forgiveness that brings about love in the sinner — like the repentant woman seeking out Jesus at the Pharisee's banquet table, loving to the point of tears and kisses because somewhere along life's roadway she came to realize she had been forgiven. And her only possible response was to love extravagantly. The issue is not whether the sinner is willing to suffer sufficient pain in order to be forgiven but rather whether the sinner's spirit is open to receiving the gift of forgiveness.

> *jesus said,*
> *"two men owed money to a certain money-lender;*
> *one owed a total of five hundred coins,*
> *the other fifty.*
> *since neither was able to repay,*
> *he wrote off both debts.*
> *which of them was more grateful to him?"*
> *simon answered, "he, i presume,*
> *to whom he remitted the larger sum."*
> *jesus said to him, "you are right."*
>
> *luke 7:36–50*

33

Two Stools instead of Three

G ROWING UP in the small town shadows of Fond du Lac, Wisconsin, during the 1950s, I spent the better part of being a kid with allergies — to cats and dogs, to pollen and house dust, to fruits and chocolate — all a cornucopia of creation that both Genesis and my instincts called "good." As best as I can remember, I was not the only kid in the neighborhood with allergies, but I probably was the only kid whose parents sent him to the allergy specialists in "big town" Milwaukee. Twice a year my father and mother would drive me to the metropolis on Lake Michigan for checkups and adjustments in the medication. By the time I was thirteen or fourteen both of them thought it would be easier if I went by myself. They would take me to the train station, check departure and arrival schedules, buy me a round-trip ticket, and promise to pick me up four or five hours later upon my return. It became a normal and uneventful routine throughout my adolescence.

Early on I had come to realize that size was not the only variable between the two cities. Fond du Lac's citizenry were white folk, all except for a black family that lived on the north side and whose father worked at Sears — all of which made Fond du Lac believe it was a modern, up-to-date, integrated city. Except that it really wasn't, for in my heart I knew that my small town womb was as prejudiced as any.

During one of my semiannual visits to the allergists, I went into the Kresege five-and-ten along Wisconsin Avenue, a few blocks from the doctors' offices. The lunch counter was crowded and only two stools remained empty — side by side, one next to a black man and one next to a white woman. Conscious of having to choose where I would sit, all of my father's teaching about the equality of all people echoed on one side, and all of the scrap metal of a society saying the opposite rattled on the other. It suddenly became a choice not of where I would sit for lunch but of where I would sit for life. I remember walking away to find another stool so that I would not have to live with the dilemma, but all the other stools were filled. I remember, too, wishing there were three stools so that I could sit in the middle. Most often, however, life does not come with such options. The reality was that I was offered two stools, the one on the right next to the black man and the one on the left next to the white woman — and no one was even aware of my turmoil. I sat on the left that day and have remembered it ever since.

It was there that I lost my innocence — at a Kresege lunch counter in downtown Milwaukee. For the first time in my life I had consciously and deliberately made a choice that crippled not only me but the two people on either side of me, as well as all those who would continue to come to that lunch counter or any other lunch counter. I had grown up fighting with my brother and talking back to my mother and lying about having done my homework, but in my young mind never before had I so clearly made a choice that so obviously stretched beyond itself. At the time, my mind could not have told the tale in such a way, yet my heart could have and did. There was something within the core of me to which I had not been faithful. There in Kresege's I entered the sinfulness of being human. And yet for some strange and unknown reason, that choice of mine was so revealing that ever since then I have found myself challenged and determined to be faithful in that one area of human life in a way seldom realized in other portions of my life.

The thread of our lives is strung with such choices for faithfulness or unfaithfulness. And while there will be those instances of unfaithfulness, in the end it is our continued faithfulness over the course of a lifetime (often becoming a journey through pain and conflict and struggle) that gives us our identity, that enables us to answer the question, "Who am I?"

Those who are faithful — to commitments, to goodness, to marriage and children and aging parents, to a hunger for justice, to the value of the human person, to truth — such folk come to know who they are. Crises of identity — adolescent or midlife or elderly — are the shadows of those who have not been faithful, who have run from life because it would be painful. They ask "Who am I?" and the windmills wave on by.

It is because we are faithful to some unknown urging to be human in its richest and fullest sense, it is because we are faithful even when our worlds are turned inside out, it is because we are faithful even when we would rather not be so, that we come to know who we are. Even when the world does not know, we know, and that is all the difference.

> *one day when jesus was praying in seclusion*
> *and his disciples were with him,*
> *he put the question to them,*
> *"who do the crowds say that i am?"*
>
> *luke 9:18–24*

34

Moments without Space

NOT HAVING YOUR OWN SPACE can be as un-American as Communism. It is the national dream and a personal prerogative, as lusted after by some as all the other "lusties" of our lives. We declare it a right and expect it to be fulfilled — our own room at home, our own office at work, our own car on the road, our own time in each day. Psychologists say healthy people have it and sick people need it. Daily runners frame it with pain and sweat, and mothers lock themselves in the bathroom just to possess it, if only for a few brief moments. Without it life would wilt, as readily as gardens without rain and children without love.

I listened to an intern tell of the emergency room in which he worked, of its shiny harmony polished each day, and of the people who marred it, disrupting it with their medical emergencies. They called them GOMERs, he said, because they wanted them to Get-Out-of-My-Emergency-Room, except that they are the very purpose hospitals have emergency rooms. Yet for some strange reason, he explained, the medical staffs looked upon those who came for emergency treatment as intruders upon the good order they worked to create, as people violating their work space. Somehow the very reasons for which emergency rooms exist tended to be seen as the enemy. The intern was not defending their attitude toward GOMERs. To the contrary, he was lamenting it and attempting to understand it in an effort to counteract it. Yet all of us want our space, and we want it nice, and we tend to want it kept that way — even when it contradicts life.

The truth is, throughout life GOMERs abound. Newcomers tip

the social balance of our friendships. Children strafe with clutter the house we just cleaned. Neat and orderly desktops become mired in last-minute muck. A simple evening of quiet and peace explodes with folks "who just thought they'd drop by for a chat." An unexpected pregnancy sabotages midlife dreams. With so many shoplifting our personal space, either "having our own space" is sacred and holy and therefore desecrated by many, or we have placed such space on high altars of idolatry, incensing it with grains of self-centered worship.

There are those, however, who do choose to live without space, who offer others entrance into their own world in such a way that there are no longer two worlds but only one. They commit themselves to a common dream, offering hope to the sisters and the brothers. Forgiving, they refuse to recognize walls and instead bridge pain. Their love survives passion and then becomes a passion for the good of all. There are such moments without space when insides touch insides and spirits sing to spirits, when all is one — like fragile color flitting in tandem with gentleness upon butterfly wings, like a summertime cone of ice cream melting both flavor and joy all over a child's smile. Such are moments not measured by distance but by the rhythm of life shared, when all worlds die and one world is born new. Not everyone finds it, because not everyone would live without a space to call one's own. But among those who do, the kingdom is now.

> *as they were making their way along,*
> *someone said to jesus,*
> *"i will be your follower wherever you go."*
> *jesus said to him, "the foxes have lairs,*
> *the birds of the sky have nests,*
> *but the son of man has nowhere to lay his head."*
>
> *luke 9:51–62*

35

On Pushing Back Fence Lines

MOMENTS OF ECSTASY usher us into a life so much bigger than ourselves, and we come away from those moments — curiously — both excited and humbled. Nighttime skies (spread eagle from eye-tip to eye-tip) seal black universes, light-speckled and vast, and then catapult us into the depth of being whole with all that is. Poets dismantle fence lines made from pickets of fear and then spin word-songs and rhythms mending all hearts into one melody. Falling in love collapses our personal worlds as we fall out of ourselves and into another. And with all of this, eternity happens — when the I who am one becomes the one who is we, when all that isolates is washed away by the wave of ecstasy that crashes over us.

We search for such moments and sort through catalogues of possible futures, hoping to find what may be the path to one more such height. I found a Sunday afternoon of such seekers not so long ago, all cast upon the grassy hills and paths of a local park. Everyone had come seeking, each for a different treasure, and yet each for the same — I suspect. A ten-year-old had brought his fishing pole to the lagoon. Blankets held those with novels as well as those hoping to sun-wash the pallor from winter-streaked bodies. A young couple roamed by, lost in the maze of paths and of hearts. Nearby a self-imagined captain of a sailing yawl navigated, via radio-control, his miniature sloop upon the ocean-lagoon and then lost control in the shallows of the island while he stood on the shore. An elderly couple shuffled past — she continually four or five steps ahead of him. I thought it strange and wondered how it came to be that over the course of fifty years they not only no longer talked but no longer even walked together. Surely they realized what had taken place, and just as surely, I suspect, they avoided discussing it. Not far away a young wife and mother, with eyes tethered to the scamperings of her little ones, had lost the power to hold her husband and could not keep her eyes from telling the tale. And I, as well, was there, watching them all. We had come, the lot of us, in quest of that day's holy grail of ecstasy, to drink from it and live for one more day.

How is it that we, who put so much energy into seeking, so seldom find? We crave to be more than our lonely selves, to overcome the very barriers we have given so much time to building for the sake of scrutiny. We desperately want to live and just as desperately fear that living will call for dying, and so we passionately explore the heights and depths of every possible experience in the hope that we may be able to conquer the barriers without death. Our society is brimming with such artificial highs, too numerous and too well known to bother noting. As if we were living on a diet of junk food, we find ourselves never really satisfied and growing less and less healthy in the process.

As is always the case, of course, the answer lies not outside us but within us. It is not a matter of discovering that which will lift us beyond the limits we have built to protect ourselves and so enter into one another. Rather it is a matter of pushing back those limits, of stretching the parameters of our lives more and more so that in the course of a lifetime all that is enters into our world. Jesus called the way of doing that *love*.

Such love does not find us — as when we fall in love. Rather it is we who find love, or perhaps it is better to say it is we who *choose* love. It is we who say "yes" to caring in such a way that in the process our whole heart beats in rhythm with all of creation, our entire spirit exists only in Spirit, our whole strength is given over to making all things new, and our entire mind shares one common vision. It is then that all neighbors and all selves become one.

> *it is not up in the sky, that you should say,*
> *"who will go up in the sky to get it for us*
> *and tell us of it, that we may carry it out?"*
> *nor is it across the sea, that you should say,*
> *"who will cross the sea to get it for us*
> *and tell us of it, that we may carry it out?"*
> *no, it is something very near to you,*
> *already in your mouths and in your hearts.*
>
> *deuteronomy 30:10–14*

36

Rainy-Day Poets

IT WAS JULY-SUMMER EVERYWHERE, dumping heat upon us as only middle-summer can do. But suddenly she turned her face on us. She who had spiked every day with heavy sun, now riddled the day with rain — and not only the day but the neighborhood and every human spirit as well. Again and again and again the rain flooded our vision until gloom became a color, until with tired anger we wanted to scratch at the clouds and rip them open like huge balloons so that they would empty their cargo and collapse — no longer able to block out the sun. Except that they were too high for us to reach. And so instead we turned to our poets — to novels and music and video tales. For so many of us, such are the poets who make life bearable, for without them we can be too easily infected with darkness.

Like Mary who found herself curled up with a listening ear among the tales of Jesus in spite of Martha's kitchen rattlings, we too need poets — not only for rainy days but also for rainy lives. We need poets just to survive. They are not a luxury but an indispensable piece of life lest we drown in drudgery or suffocate in stale routine. We need mystery writers and songsters, storytellers with film and with book, television and video, CDs and concerts — all poets of one kind or another. They help us unravel the knots in our hearts and serve us hope when hunger hurts.

Rainbow Summer is a Milwaukee, Monday-through-Friday collection of assorted poets — free noontime concerts of chamber music, mime, folk, country, comic, symphony, dance, sing-a-long. Surrounded by a grove of chestnut trees along the Milwaukee

River, these outdoor concerts have become a lunchtime picnic for the city's downtown business district. I go down there occasionally, partly to listen to the "poet of the day" and partly just to watch the folks who gather.

What continues to amaze me is the construction workers and tradesfolk who gather from the building sites and are captivated by the performances and the music. A bit shamefacedly, I confess my bias that blue collar-workers would show a preference for Springsteen's *Born in the U.S.A.* and be indifferent to Vivaldi's *Four Seasons*. Not so, I have come to realize, as I watched those who labor to re-create the shape of the city come with lunchbox and thermos and be enthralled with that day's string quartet or lite piano. There is a common thread within the human fabric that responds to beauty — both to the sublime in Vivaldi as well as to the wrenchingly human in Springsteen, to the comic who is able to turn our insides with laughter as well as to the dancer who captures our awe with movement and rhythm.

The business day would continue to turn about the sun whether Rainbow Summer marked the noon hours or not, I am sure. Yet is it too naive to wonder if because of Rainbow Summer some family seeking a home loan might be treated with a bit more compassion, or to hope that some contract might be written more conscious of the need for justice, or to believe that some high rise might shine with one more ray of gleam because its laborers had constructed it not only with sweat and pain but also with a smile of satisfaction in recognition of its beauty? Such is the fruit of poetry cast upon the human spirit; such is the work of story and song and image and word.

Leo Lionni wrote *Frederick*, a child's story about a field mouse who daydreamed worlds and absorbed life while all the others worked to store up reserves for winter's menu of cold and snow. Frederick was roundly criticized until winter's boredom outlived all of their reserves. It was then, midway through the dreary season, that Frederick's tales of play and memories of summer sun and fields of beauty brought life to all the others.

Like Martha our hands are full with each day's table tasks, and yet like Mary, we find ourselves with still another kind of hunger in need of being fed. To such folk came Jesus, with dreams of the kingdom and hints of resurrection and promises yet to be unraveled — all too absurd to be believed, yet all giving word to the hope with which we continually live. And such, we have come to believe, is the better portion of our human spirit.

"only one thing is required.
mary has chosen the better portion
and she shall not be deprived of it."

luke 10:38–42

37

Even without Asking

W E ALL HAVE NEEDS OF ONE SORT OR ANOTHER — some of them
real and some perceived, but all of them needs, nonetheless.
What we indeed do not need are more needs. Whichever fairy
godmother or celestial archangel has been assigned to dispensing
needs has been most generous — perhaps even a bit extravagant.
We have needs for time and health and money and job, hungers for
love and forgiveness, yearnings for the good life or the fast-paced
fun life or sometimes just for more life.

Over the years one of the more time-honored ways of satisfying
those needs has come to be prayer. Having been assured that God
will not give us a snake if we ask for a fish or a scorpion if we ask for
an egg, we piously telegram the hungers of our lives to whatever
distant deity might be currently on the listening end — all of this
despite the fact that many often find themselves with a snake in
their throat or a scorpion in their grasp, with illness as they go about
seeking health or jobless as they continually struggle to raise their
family. Yet we play to God with our prayers.

When I was a freshman or sophomore in high school, I remember my mother became very seriously ill. It had something to do
with her thyroid, the doctors said, and they did not know whether
or not she would recover. It is a child's worse fear that a parent
might die, and in so many ways I was still a child then. I remember
praying feverishly for her recovery and somewhere in the process
making a bargain with God that if she recovered I would pray a
rosary every day for the rest of my life. She did recover, though I
now doubt it had anything to do with my bargain. Nevertheless,

upon her recovery I began to carry out the terms I had set, and every day I spent the ten or fifteen minutes it took praying the rosary. It must have been a year or so later that the monotony and discipline of that daily rosary began to cause my commitment to fray. I remember deciding then that God could not be bought with promises and that therefore my contract would not be binding after all. Fortunately for my own psyche, my mother's health continued strong and well for another thirty years despite my reneging on God.

Some twenty-five years later my father became seriously ill due to a tumor on the brain, which the doctors diagnosed as malignant and terminal. Eventually that initial diagnosis proved to be inaccurate and the surgery showed the tumor to be benign, enabling a satisfactory recovery for my father. Yet during that slice of days between the first and second diagnosis, I strangely never found myself praying for his recovery, though such was what I deeply and painfully desired. Instead I found myself living with a sense that whatever would be would be, and that life could still be whole, regardless of the outcome. It was not that God was absent. If anything, God was more fully present, and so I sensed no need to ask.

I have often wondered what happened in that span of twenty-five years that made me shift from pleading and bargaining over life to being able to live with life. When did that happen? And why did that happen? I suppose none of that really matters, only that it happened. Somewhere in their telling, however, our lives do seem to get reversed, or maybe it is simply that the characters switch roles, and we find ourselves answering our own questions or struggling to complement our own deeds.

In time our own story does become the Jesus-tale of the midnight neighbor who insists on rousing a sleeping neighborhood for bread so that he might feed a midnight friend coming to visit. And the family next door, already lost in dreams, must wake to the nightmare of getting up and feeding their neighbor's hunger for bread, but then also discovering that in doing so they are feeding as well their own hunger for some peace and quiet and sleep — all because that midnight neighbor wouldn't go away. It is, of course, the story of how we persistently plague God with our prayers for daily bread, believing that God will eventually give in — only to discover by the end of our lives that it is rather the story of how God persistently plagues us for entry into our own bolted lives, and not vice versa. And thus finally at the end of our living it is we who feed God's passion to be loved.

When does it all happen that the characters of life switch roles? It doesn't matter so much *when*, I suppose — only that it happens and that we come to recognize it.

> *jesus said to his disciples,*
> *"when you pray, say:*
> *'father,*
> *hallowed be your name,*
> *your kingdom come.'"*
>
> *luke 11:1–13*

38

Shook Foil

SOMEWHERE ALONG ITS WESTERN RIM the Great Lake Michigan brushes past Milwaukee and beaches itself at Klode Park and then northward for a sandy stretch of perhaps an eye's distance or more. I wandered there not so long ago with no other purpose than to wander, I suppose, but maybe as well to let the waves wash an anxious day as they also washed the beach. It was a lonely sort of pass with little to befriend the beach except for scattered driftwood and casual footprints mapping a path or two.

Two figures marked the distance, and as I came to pass on by I saw them to be two youths, a boy and girl no more than fifteen or so. Knee deep in the water, he stood there wearing a swimming suit as well as a baseball cap turned front to back with a spray of blondish hair over his forehead where the plastic band adjusts to size. With a somber gaze and arms folded, he stared out over the water, though I must admit it was his somber back turned to her that first caught my attention. Brandishing a "Hard Rock Cafe" logo on the front of her knee-length T-shirt, she matched his gaze with the same lost and distant look as she leaned against a rock ten or fifteen yards behind him.

I wouldn't have bothered noticing except that it all appeared so strange — these two young folk who had come to the beach to share a good time with one another, only to find themselves not talking to one another, not looking at one another, not even standing beside one another. What had they said or done to recipe such forlorn wondering? What happened or did not happen or happened that should not have happened?

Whatever it was, they had the appearance of having come into some new and unexpected time — a try-to-understand look as if a world had opened that they never knew existed and from which there was no turning back, like a blacksmith's crafting, fired and hammered into some new shape and then sealed there forever with a plunge into a watery pool. The looks on their faces and the terribly lonely stances they each took seemed to tell the tale of somehow being changed and yet not really sure what it was that made them so, or if they even wanted it. It is so often mystery that puts us in such a stance, washing over our blindness and allowing us to see as if for the first time, even if only a glimpse — yet in such a way that we are no longer the same.

We do trip over mystery, and then glimpse that life is not lived at the surface in everyday dabblings, but that something of stirring significance is occurring beneath those dabblings — and our seeing is little more than a hunch, like the windshield of our world shattered by a stone from some passing world, leaving a cracked and disjointed view of whatever is. And we hunger for it all the more without even knowing what it is for which we hunger — except to know that it must be more than what seems to be. That is how it is with mystery.

It is that same hunger that lures us into the thrill of a roller coaster, sensing that in some controlled but daring way we can flirt with the mystery of death and all its curiosity and yet return home safe. It is that same hunger that teases us into gently coaxing a butterfly to settle on our shoulder because we want to believe that the mystery of trust just may be able to bridge the gaps of creation. It is that same hunger, as well, that urges us out of bed to watch a sunrise or catches us cooing and babbling at a new born baby — simply because we want to hope that the mystery of a new beginning may brush us with new life and possibility as well. It is mystery in those moments, shining brilliant — like shook foil, to borrow a phrase from Hopkins. It is mystery that transforms us and transfigures us all into something only a little less than gods because we are more than dabblings on the surface of a bumbling world. It *is* mystery after all that is none other than God.

jesus took peter, john, and james,
and went up onto a mountain to pray.
while he was praying,
his face changed in appearance
and his clothes became dazzlingly white.

luke 9:28–36
transfiguration

39

Lost Kingdoms

I COULDN'T HELP BUT WONDER why the boat out on the lake had become so important to him — except that it obviously had. There were three of us milling about the beach's concession stand while the soda jerk who seemed slower than usual just kept on taking his time making sodas. So the three of us simply continued shuffling from one foot to the other, looking out over the lake, and waiting for our turn in line. Out on the lake a couple hundred yards from shore, a sail boat made its way parallel to the shore, only it was not under sail. Despite a somewhat stiff breeze, the boat was moving along under its own power, and this upset him. He had gathered at least sixty years of living as he stood there, mustached and pot-bellied. Like a cookie jar with handles, he kept his hands stuffed in the pockets of his denim shorts all the while brushing his space with his handlebar arms. He would stare out over the water, then turn away, and then come back to gaze some more, all the while mumbling first to the other waiting with me and then to me, mumbling about how foolish it was to motor a boat when the wind could do just as well and maybe even better. "Look at that," he would say, biting the words, first to one of us and then to the other. "It just doesn't make sense. No, it doesn't. Why doesn't he use his sail? It's all sort of crazy." Then he would turn away, only to come back and wonder aloud all over again. It was the soda jerk who finally broke the rhythm and shortened the line to two.

I wondered why a person would become so irritated over someone else's boat and choice of power. It seemed so foolish to be upset, and yet it wasn't foolish for fully a third of those of us in line. Probably little different, I later mused, than growing angry over failing to attain straight As, or a son's or daughter's choice of mate or profession, or a spouse who forgets to fill the tank with gas. Yes, you say, but some things matter more than others. Obviously. Obviously. That is why some grow angry and others do not.

The angers of our lives do set us off on any number of end runs, and in the process we find (usually too late) that we have missed a portion of life — or at least a sunny day at the beach. We missed Christmas because Uncle Alex drank too much and ruined the dinner with everyone's arguing. Or we missed Katie's first steps because of our frustrated temper over a video camera we were unable to get to record. Or we missed love because of the way someone squeezed a tube of toothpaste. The events of life and love and joy break open moments when life reigns full and plenty, when we sense that we are given all the treasures and riches to be had — equal to all the kingdoms and queendoms of the earth. Tragedies do not occur when we lose those kingdoms and queendoms (as if, indeed, they *could* be lost) for they are always present in varying fashion. No, tragedies occur when we miss the kingdom because of angers or preoccupations or misfed hungers — sometimes without even knowing it. Such was the constant worry of Jesus. His heart ached because people failed to recognize a kingdom already given.

If there is any awareness needed among human beings, it is not a cautious preparation for some cosmic turn-around charioted in on a Santa Claus sleigh of heavenly cloud. On the contrary, the awareness to which he kept calling us is a sensitivity for the present, to be constantly prepared to recognize a kingdom already in our midst — like beauty in a dandelion, or hope in the obnoxious teenager, or a change of heart brought on by illness. The kingdom is everywhere, yet undoubtedly least recognized.

> *jesus said to his disciples:*
> *"do not live in fear, little flock.*
> *it has pleased your father to give you the kingdom.*
> *... let your belts be fastened around your waists*
> *and your lamps be burning ready."*
>
> *luke 12:32–48*

40

Sort of Like Owen Meaney

"GOD HAS A REASON FOR EVERYTHING," explain the sooth-sayers, only in varying fashion depending upon the circumstances. When an aging family member necessitates constant and tedious care, the wisdom-spin is "God never gives more than one can bear." Or in the instance of a tragedy avoided by shear happenstance, we recognize that "her time had not yet come." Or when a random assortment of occurrences unexpectedly and inexplicably culminates in some tragedy, well "that's the way it was meant to be." It seems that each of us human beings, who have ourselves been dipped and saturated in mystery, have our own need to experience mystery, not only at times seeing mystery where there may be none, but also providing an explanation so that the mystery itself then disintegrates.

I supposed I tend to be a bit skeptical of such facile unravelings, and while I am not sure why life comes at us the way it does, I'm hesitant to simply conclude that "God wanted it that way," as if it were all part of some master plan. Yet when I finished reading John Irving's novel, *A Prayer for Owen Meaney*, I found myself wondering if, just maybe, they could be right and I wrong. It is the story of Owen Meaney's life and how all its strange and obscure pieces come together — his premature birth and consequently his squeaky premature voice, his basketball ability to stuff the basket despite a five foot height, the quirky fate of his military career, all strewn with bizarre dreams and even a vision or two. Yet it all is finally assembled, though admittedly with the pen of fiction, in such a way as to have made we wonder, "Maybe they're right."

There is really no way of knowing, however, and so the quandary remains like a lonely shadow in a flatland desert.

If God has anything to say about how it all comes together, it may very well be said in the resurrection. Everything does come together, and it does so at the point of death, and we call it Life. Beyond that, I'm not sure there is much else to say — simply Life. And all those other coincidences? Well, I just don't know — or care, I suppose. However they find themselves assembled really doesn't matter much — Owen Meaney or not.

> *just as in adam all die,*
> *so in christ all will come to life again,*
> *but each one in proper order:*
> *christ the first fruits and then, at his coming,*
> *all those who belong to him.*
>
> *1 corinthians 15:20–26*
> *assumption*

41

A Touch of Fire

SOMEWHERE IN THE COURSE OF OUR LIVES, each of us has to do what we have to do because it is the right thing to do, and the only satisfaction may very well be knowing that we did the right thing. It is often such moments that no one else understands because they do not see the entire picture, or know what we know, or have to live the life we must. And so worlds flame with anger and burn with resentment because we do not seem to see or hear or believe as everyone else does — except that we see and hear and believe only too well. And so we do what we must do, and the only satisfaction is knowing that we did the right thing.

One day we find the courage to talk to a teacher about a friend on drugs. Or we can no longer run away from living for ourselves and so accept the fact that we have to give two years of our life to the Peace Corps. Or we tell our parents we are gay. Or we admit that alcohol has ruined our life. Or we say aloud to our spouse, "I'm not happy and we have to make this marriage better." Or we walk away from a job that has been compromising our principles. Or we are honest with someone, perhaps for the first time. Or we let ourselves cry. Or we end a relationship that has no future and has been destructive of ourselves as well as of the other person. Or a million other "whatevers" that may make us who we are — whether we like them or not. And so we do what we have to do, whether anyone understands or not.

It is at such moments, I suspect, that we discover who we are, or perhaps become who we were meant to become. And should we

133

cringe or shrink from such reality, we will forever remain stunted, lost in a maze of "should have's".

When I was younger I think I faced such moments and such choices more readily. I don't mean when I was a child, but when I had just *begun* being an adult — or maybe I just remember them more clearly because those were the first times, and first loves always stay with us. Yet it seems my choices then were more clearly fence-line choices — not fence *sitting*. In the yard or out. Choose a world or a dream or some grassy playground, but choose. That was how I lived then, when life seemed black-and-white. Then someone along the way began to remind me that life is mostly gray and not so black-and-white. And so it seems my choices are not as self-determining now — as if they might be only hollow wishes in which spirit ricochets and echoes until its energy is spent.

Maybe it is because we learn to make choices that are more polished, smoother or sanded at the edges so not as many people are offended. In the end, then, I suppose we find ourselves taking stands without having to take a stand. We do the right thing even when it is offensive, but we learn how to do it in a palatable way so that it does not seem offensive. But then maybe it ceases to be right as well. I think what we do then is take the fire out of life, the passion that must burn for there to be light.

Equus, a bizarre tale told after the fact while the protagonist lies on a psychologist's couch, is about a young adolescent who blinded a stable of horses because of sexual conflict and tension and love. It is really a story of coming to understand and to accept who one is, a tale of healing that takes place during its telling. So at the end of the telling, the now older adolescent finds a way to live in his present and be at peace with his past, though not without cost. The drive, the passion, the energy that fueled his life have found a way to lie dormant in some quiet, psychic niche. And the psychologist then comes face to face with the dilemma of whether healing at the expense of passion makes a person more human or less. Does life without fire in fact die for lack of light?

> *jesus said to his disciples:*
> *"i have come to light a fire on the earth.*
> *how I wish the blaze were ignited."*
>
> luke 12:49–53

42

The Shell Game

MUCH OF OUR LIVES is spent exploring ways into whatever it is we need to get into. We seek a way into the college of our choice; or we look for ways into the right corporation; or we make our way from real estate agent to real estate agent in order to find a home in the right neighborhood. We hope to fall into love, or marry into the proper family, or break into a circle of friends. We wait in line to get into a store for the sale it is holding, and then later on we stand at our front door with arms full of packages and fumble for a house key so that we can get into the inside and out of the outside. We wait to get into the elevator and then wait to get out of the elevator so we can find our way into our office. And of course, who of us has not known the frustration of trying to get into a bag of potato chips hermetically sealed in plastic.

For most of us, somewhere between the college of our choice and the bag of potato chips, it also dawns on us that we need to find our way into the kingdom of heaven. We fear finding ourselves standing outside the locked and narrow door gazing in upon all those lasts who have somehow become firsts while we realize that we who thought we just may have been good enough to be among the firsts have in fact become, if not last, at least outside rather than inside. And every once in a while such wondering comes upon us forcefully enough to make us stop and think about it twice before we go back to the hermetically sealed life with which we are struggling. One might almost conclude that, in some quixotic fashion, we might be better off sinning and trying to be evil and thereby also last, so that when the tables do get turned (as Jesus continually seems to suggest they will) we will be made first. It does seem that faith and life can indeed be a shell game in which winning is all but impossible — which may very well be the narrow door incapable of being earned.

Most of the time the narrow door opens before us, and all we need do is step through — which is another way of saying that life comes with all sorts of twists and turns inviting us to walk its path, except that often enough we would rather not. Much of the time we would prefer to live life without acned futures and disappointed loves and children who fight growing up because it is not the life Howdy Doody promised. And so we continually look for doors or archways or four-lane avenues into some other daydream. Left to itself, however, life will usher us into the kingdom if only we live it as it comes. Its soap-opera episodes will make us gentle or forgiving or patient or whatever else it is with which we need to be tempered. If it is narrow, it is only because we would rather not walk it.

The marvelous contradiction is that one need not be a believer to enter the kingdom. The narrow door of life is there for everyone to live it. The reason faith is such a gift is that it alerts us to that magnificent reality, lest we become lost in the maze of dead-end choices like some white mouse confused by all the alternatives. Then they who thought themselves to be first through the maze find themselves lost as well as last, and those who were thought to be last simply because they plodded through reality find themselves first, winning not only the pea under the right shell but the shell and all of the rest of life as well.

> someone asked jesus,
> "lord, are they few in number
> who are to be saved?"
> he replied:
> "try to come in through the narrow door.
> many, i tell you, will try to enter
> and be unable.
> some who are last will be first
> and some who are first will be last.
>
> luke 13:22–30

43

The Anger of Pride

I FOUND I WAS ANGRY AT MYSELF THE OTHER DAY, as we all do, I suppose, whenever we put our foot in our mouth or forget about an important engagement or scramble whatever it was we had hoped would be picture perfect. What I had scrambled this time was a homily. For some reason or other the image came out wrong, or the example did not fit, or it just did not come together the way I had hoped. And I was angry with myself — to the point that it caught me off guard, like a sudden noise startling the quiet, only this time it was an unexpected glimpse that startled the noise of my busyness. What it did was point out the fact that the way people might perceive me as a preacher had taken on more importance than the preaching — than the Word itself. Life had gotten out of focus, I suppose. A perspective had been lost — or perhaps exchanged for another — and, as with the turn of a kaleidoscope, life took on a different image, only this time other than the one intended.

In happens to us all in the course of our lifetimes — and more than once. We adjust the perspective and set ourselves up for the fall. Grades become more important than the learning, or being right more important than the relationship, or the label of greater worth than the clothing. It happens between parent and child, as it did in the film *Dead Poets Society*, when a son's or daughter's profession is of greater significance to the parent than is that son's or daughter's happiness. Like the parable of Jesus, where we sit at table takes on greater meaning than the people who gather or the meal that is shared.

That is what pride does. It distorts what is real and shifts the focus of life upon ourselves — and in the process redefines who we are. Our identity then comes from our grades or our labels or our children or our preaching or whatever tiara it is that we have chosen to wear. And when that tiara falls, as always tiaras do, so do we. Distorted worth brings distorted failure. Perhaps that is, then, the greatest tragedy accompanying pride — that in the end we destroy ourselves. We, who once thought our worth came from our strengths and our gifts, think ourselves worthless when the strengths turn to weaknesses and the gifts to curses.

In the Christian tradition it is our gathering for Eucharist that keeps the balance, or at least the vision. If nowhere else, it must at least be at the Lord's Table that we are able to come together as equals, as brothers and sisters finding identity in one another and not in ourselves or our labors — despite all the impulses to the contrary. Our communities may be sliced by a racial knife; our society may have strafed the poor in order to bankroll the wealthy; our church may have sacrificed the gifts of her daughters for the sake of male power. Yet the vision that continually gathers us is that of the meal at which all are equal, in spite of the contradictions we consciously or unconsciously live. Some would say it is hypocrisy, and others an attempt to calm a guilty conscience. And that may be. But it is also the light kept burning in the darkness. And then as long as it burns and as often as we gather, hope will not be snuffed out for we will continually be challenged to keep life focused and to level those mountains and chasms of our own making that divide us.

> *jesus went on to address a parable to the guests:*
> *"when you are invited by someone*
> *to a wedding party,*
> *do not sit in the place of honor*
> *in case some greater dignitary has been invited.*
> *then the host might come and say to you,*
> *'make room for this man,'*
> *and you would have to proceed shamefacedly*
> *to the lowest place."*
>
> *luke 14:1, 7–14*

44

A Surcharge for Living

THERE IS A TIME FOR US when life explodes with flashy color like Fourth of July "boomers" in rapid succession — cannons pounding not only our eardrums and chests with thumping shock waves but also our everyday living. It begins for most of us, I think, when we turn sixteen and get our driver's license, which is to say it begins with coming to know some freedom and independence in our lives. And that time continues on through all sorts of valleys and hills until it reaches the distant terminal that is probably that time when our jobs or our marriages lose their novelty and settle into some sort of expected routine. The in between is scattered with insights and discoveries and vials of excitement and sometimes disappointments. But it is in these years that life turns new for us — our first car, moving away from home, the dance of falling into love and out of love and over again, the dazzle of college and perhaps even of learning, the pains of winning and losing and ultimately of compromising, unearthing gifts and talents and self-worth, the challenge of naming the future for ourselves both with fear as well as with intrigue. All of it explodes in the span of a decade or so, and all of it with the illusion that we are making the choices free for the taking.

There is a cost, of course — a surcharge for living tacked on well after life has begun being used and can no longer be returned. I have heard too many folk ask who would marry if they knew what marriage would demand, and they ask it with a carbonated voice turned flat. Or the toll exacted from raising a family — for many it should rather be a dowry received. Or the price of wisdom — it is never worth the sum of pain until, of course, the healing comes and often with that healing the scars that stamp the bill "paid." Life is never free of charge, yet worse than that — the cost is always hidden.

On a Sunday afternoon I watched two families come to the park to spend the day. They came to the top of a high, grassy hill that sloped to the lake far below. The one family (a father and five children tucked with a picnic lunch and assorted frisbees) immediately responded to the hill's invitation. They rolled and cartwheeled their way down, and laughed and giggled their way back up, only to turn it again and again. The other family (a mom and a dad and a Jimmy aged five tucked with energy but also with assorted cautions) sat and watched. Jimmy caught the enthusiasm of the others, but his mom's warnings of grass stains and fears of a broken neck strained to control the energy. And she succeeded in the control, but at the cost of a fun-filled memory of family play, at the cost of going home in tears. Costs do often come hidden in our choices.

Most often the cost *is* in the cake, or in the eating of it when its worth is also in the having. But it can't be both. Among the annals of religious telling, it is said that before the birth of Buddha the shaman told his father that the Buddha would be either the greatest and most powerful leader the people would ever have or he would be the holiest and wisest spirit among the ordinary and common folk. Life can be that way — either/or, but not both. One excludes the other — and hence the cost.

Strangely enough, however, the price of believing varies from gathering to gathering. The cost for Catholics is a Sunday morning in bed along with the added tax of birth control for those before the age of fifty or so. For Adventists it is the use of alcohol and tobacco; and for the Christian Science it is the healing skills of modern medicine. Amish, on the other hand, surrender gasoline, while Jehovah's Witnesses sacrifice blood transfusions. The list begins to grow a bit absurd and makes one wonder how it is that Jesus' command to simply love came to be translated so differently in so many languages of faith. Perhaps the cost of love grows too great for us and perhaps too endless as well.

if one of you decides to build a tower,
will he not first sit down
and calculate the outlay
to see if he has enough money
to complete the project?
he will do that for fear of laying the foundation
and then not being able to complete work;
at which all who saw it
would then jeer at him, saying,
"that man began to build what he could not finish."

luke 14:25–33

45

Home among Us Drifters

THE PARISH MAINTENANCE MAN knocked on the open door of my office the other day and stuck his head in. He laid out all the options in rapid succession, as he always does — I think because he wants to keep me happy and hopes I will pick from his assortment with the thought that whichever one I choose is his only recommended suggestion. The issue this time was a local drifter sleeping between the buildings and leaving an empty bottle or two behind in the morning. Duane was wondering *what* to do about him or *if* to do about him or *should* to do about him — and I was about to say "yes" to the "should do about him," except that Duane's baker's dozen of options slipped in a few words about "not bothering anyone" followed by an immediate "move him along" and "shouldn't be there" — just to cover all the bases. And for some reason or other I was listening closer than I sometimes do and was snagged by the "not bothering anyone" as if Duane was thinking it was maybe okay to let the drifter stay there. And of course Duane was right, except that I would not have thought about it, except that Duane did and said so. And so we did. We let the drifter stay.

It later came to pass that the drifter had really drifted on home — home to us, that is. You see, though he was forty years old now, he had once gone to grade school here. He had lived in this neighborhood, learned how to read in the rooms above his current playground bed, stood in line for a drink at these very corridor "bubblers," and memorized his times tables here long before his life had multiplied to what it is now. Here too he had made his First Communion, learned about Jesus, and been told that God loves him. And having perhaps forgotten that, something nevertheless drew him back to hear it once again.

There is a sadness in all of that which somehow became much more real when Duane told me the drifter's history. I mean, how is it that a child chucked full of dreams of growing up and being important, dreams of being a baseball star or a hero or one of the "big people" on Hampton Avenue, how is it that such dreams are siphoned off only to leave what some would call the dregs? Except that it happens in human life — in others' as well as in ours. It is not always so catastrophic, so world crushing. More frequently we compromise our dreams in lesser ways. We choose to be less than what we could have been and short circuit the energy in our lives — only to fry our own goodness. What we do is we sin.

I confess that it was much easier to live with "Sr. Dontila sin" in the fourth grade than it is to face in myself that real sin that dismantles who I am. Grade-school commandments that handcuffed dirty thoughts and sibling skirmishes were tolerable. The fragments of conscience that confront my comfort and indifference, my willingness to concede that life is not lived at the surface but rather *beneath* that "safe" zone where I must unwrap the honesty, that is where I find sin because that is where I squander myself upon my pleasures or fears or contentment. That is where I become nobody.

I don't know if that home-grown drifter continues to cover himself with the shadows of our buildings. He may well have moved on by now to other climes and other pasts. What lingers still, however, is that my first impulse was to suggest that he move on, as though he had no right to come back home, and that may have been more of an undoing for me than his being lost was for him. We all have different homes to which we must return, and sometimes the longest journey is a turn of the heart.

> the elder son said in reply to his father:
> "for years now i have slaved for you.
> i never disobeyed one of your orders,
> yet you never gave me so much as a kid goat
> to celebrate with my friends.
> then, when this son of yours returns
> after having gone through your property
> with loose women,
> you kill the fatted calf for him."
>
> luke 15:1–32

46

A Plan for Goodness
along Green Bay Avenue

GREEN BAY AVENUE SLITS MY WORLD, stretching itself past the front of our house and reaching in either direction for about as far as you might care to go on most days. Last summer the movers and the shakers came and made Green Bay Avenue new with curbs and boulevards and asphalt so smooth you could roller skate on it without having to worry about cracks and bumps. And when the movers and the shakers left, others came and planted trees and sod and islands of color. And everyone said how much nicer Green Bay Avenue was, only I am not sure anyone now remembers the difference — come a year later.

There is no way of knowing, of course, what folks think about as they drive by or what they talk about to one another, but I would wager hardly anyone ever comments about how much nicer Green Bay Avenue is today. Most of us, I suspect, simply think about getting to wherever it is we need to get. Traffic is somewhat faster now, and so the local constabulary hides along the way in order to slow us down. And the potholes that turned the road into a pinball journey from side to side and bumper to bumper, well, they are only memories for a cocktail party now when conversation lags and the night gets long. In the meantime Green Bay Avenue ushers people on with an unnoticed flair — on into their lives or their futures or perhaps even on into some sort of goodness unthought of and unplanned.

That is how it is with our goodness. As much as we might want to be good, and most of us do want to be good — for we do not like ourselves very well when we are not so good, when we are cranky or selfish or lazy or not so honest — so as much as we want to be good, for the most part we just let it happen or presume it will on its own. We rush down Green Bay Avenue or Vliet Street or Capitol Drive or Washington Boulevard or whatever roadway our lives happen to be traveling at the moment — and maybe we rush into goodness and maybe we don't. And that is where the tragedy lies. Maybe we don't.

My mother always worried that I would miss the goodness. So she was always insisting (as most mothers do) that I not fight with my brother, and that he and I not scream at each other (or what might the neighbors think?), and that I stay out of Mrs. Henning's yard (even if it meant losing my baseball to her garden), and that I never talk back to grown-ups, and that I not say "shut up" or "I hate you" to anyone. Goodness was programmed then, and I grew to hate the programming (though hating *that* was all right as long as one did not hate people).

Maybe that is why most of us tend to *drift* through life and hopefully into goodness. We tend not to plan our goodness because too much of life is planned out for us and often with too much detail — education, wedding celebrations, social gatherings, vacations, even who gets up first in the morning to get the bathroom. Some things need to be left to chance, if only to be able to survive. And so for all these reasons and others as well, we tend not to plan how to grow good.

Yet maybe we should, and every once in a while somewhere along Green Bay Avenue we do think about it. We think about the fact that we need to forgive Harry or be patient with the kids or be a little understanding of the secretary or listen to the lonely neighbor next door. And we decide to do it. And maybe that is the best we can do — given all the other "have to's" with which we live. And so we do plan our goodness, then, though most of the time in bits and pieces. But that's okay. That is how we grow into love, too, in bits and pieces.

the owner then gave his devious employee
credit for being enterprising!
why?
because the worldly take more initiative
than the otherworldly
when it comes to dealing with their own kind.

luke 16:1–13

47

Like Tomato Plants and Boiling Frogs

IT WON'T BE LONG NOW, and one of these nights soon the killing frost will come, only it won't come killing. It'll just come settling in, which is how most dying comes anyway — just settling in. And in the morning everyone will know. The impatiens will have turned to greeny slime, and the tomato plants will have lost their courage and just given up, and most everything else will have simply wilted as if God or Mother Nature or the Tooth Fairy or whoever it was who was in charge during the night simply snapped the rubber band wrapped around the cover of the night with such a loud crack that everyone was frightened into white death. Only everyone will say it was a killing frost because it is so much easier to explain that way. And so will come the end of one more growing season, but also the end of one more dying season — which is one and the same, because, of course, growing is really about bearing fruit and bearing fruit is what dying is all about, unless, of course, what one means by dying is simply to cease being.

The world around my neighborhood is not the same after a killing frost. The woods walk differently — a bit more distant, I would say. And the colors, well, it is as if someone had blackened them a touch — not a lot, mind you, but just enough to take the edge off their brilliance. The wind seems more daring, too, with something of a bite to it, as if someone had left the door unlatched and let it run free and untethered for the first time. Suddenly, with one spin of the moon, my world is changed. Death does that when it comes and settles in.

One of the kids left his science book here on the dining room table the other day, and before he came back to pick it up I paged through it — simply to see what science was about these days. Page 121 was all about environment and spoke of it in terms of frogs — as in a frog that is dropped into boiling water immediately and instinctively jumps out, whereas a frog placed into tap water and then brought to a boil simply stays and dies — which is the science book's way of recognizing that death in most instances tends to simply settle in. We tend not to notice until the abyss is so great that there is no going back, not to life nor back to before the killing frost because once death has settled in there is nothing more but death.

Such was the story of the rich man dressed in fine purple who everyday walked past Lazarus dressed only in sores, and not only past Lazarus but past his own future as well. And he did it in such a way that he never noticed how the killing frost was settling in, until it had, of course, and then there was no going back. Some will say that the rich man never deserved what he got, that he never deserved the abyss because he did not realize what was happening (or what was settling in) — except that realizing it *never* matters, not to tomato plants or to frogs or even to rich men. It happens anyway, whether we recognize it or not, and then we live with it — which is a strange way to talk about dying.

Have you ever noticed how we hesitate to name something sin? We do not like doing it. We are willing to label this or that as wrong, but to place it in the category of sin — well, we simply refuse to do so. I could name a half dozen reasons why — such as not wishing to judge or not being able to read another's heart — and they all make sense and are a portion of the answer, I am sure. But more than any of these, I have come to think that we simply do not want to believe that what we do today has any effect upon how we will live tomorrow. We want to believe that a huge abyss separates one day from another so that nothing can cross over, and thus we can be free from the consequences of our choices. We refuse to forgive and do not want to understand that that is why we live lonely lives, or we prefer to pay for security with capital punishment and want to be able to continue wondering why life is cheap on drug-strewn streets. Death does settle in, then, not unlike the killing frost, and in the morning we gaze across the emptiness and wonder how we got to where we are. Death does that to us when it comes and settles in.

> *"my child," replied abraham,*
> *"remember that you were well off in your lifetime,*
> *while lazarus was in misery.*
> *now he has found consolation here,*
> *but you have found torment.*
> *and that is not all.*
> *between you and us there is fixed a great abyss."*
>
> luke 16:19–31

48

Like Peanut Butter, Like Death

I HAVE ALWAYS THOUGHT that if the Fairy Godmother finally does come to my nighttime dreams and offers me three free wishes, I know what one of them will be — to be Neil Diamond for one lifetime, or maybe even for just one evening. Now why Neil Diamond and not Bruce Springsteen or Barbara Streisand or Randy Travis, I am not sure — except that it has always been my fantasy to stand before twenty thousand people, all enthralled by my diamonds of song.

Last summer at a picnic gathering, if it was not the Fairy Godmother who came, it was at least her assistant. Someone brought their tape system with almost every imaginable song recorded in instrumental, and we who had gathered were invited to dub the lyrics. My Andy Warhol moment of fame was about to materialize as I stepped onto the stage of idolized reverence. The track of *Sweet Caroline* began. My voice opened to song. And I, in disbelief, lost the rhythms and then the melody and finally my fantasy. I bombed and my dream died.

Like too much of a peanut butter sandwich, death always swallows hard — whether in small things or big, whether at play or at life, whether in dreams or in the stuff of what is real. Even for autumn, who lives with her better than anyone else, death goes down hard. Then the eaves on our roofs choke on rain-licked leaves, and even the gutters in the street cannot swallow all the leftover color shed by the dying season. Some will say it is the letting go that makes death so difficult. I should rather think it is the fact that, having let go, there is nothing so obvious to grab onto. Like kids on the playground swinging from rung to rung on an overhead ladder, it is the "inbetween" at which we panic when for a moment we swing through life without knowing if we will make it to the next rung, without knowing if indeed death does free us for life. And so we panic at the thought of falling. Death swallows hard.

We look for antidotes to ease the pain then, for a glass of milk with which to swallow the peanut butter, thinking that if we only had enough faith, life might go a bit more to our liking. Indeed, if faith the size of a tiny seed can play the gardener and transplant trees into the sea, why not also calm our ulcers, still our worrisome fears, find us a job, or even enable us to be Neil Diamond for a day. And so we conclude we must need more faith for we cannot even spark our dreams or defuse the struggle of one ordinary day, much less reforest the ocean.

In the meantime, however, we continue threading day after day upon a chain of lifetime. We love and make love in spite of our ulcers; laughter is somehow able to bubble up through our worries and fears; and peanut butter and jelly sandwiches sustain us for beauty just as well as lobster and steak once did when we had a job. We enter into life as best as we can, and in the process discover that life enters into us. And that is when faith takes place, and more than a seed's worth. There in that moment we come to realize that we have no need to transplant trees into the sea. There is enough of faith for life.

Whenever we live life as it comes, committed to doing what must be done, faith happens. When we homework our way through first grade for the second time only this time beside our own child, when we return each day to the oppressive routine of a monotonous job and we do it for no other reason than our family's needs, when we listen our way through the repetitious tales of yesteryear and smile with interest at each of them, when we forgive the same hurt time after time after time, when we live and work the double duty of being a single parent — in the midst of all these and much else besides, we find ourselves becoming people of faith; and for some reason or other it is enough faith to meet our God. It may not be enough to make me Neil Diamond or you financially solvent, but then such is not the purpose of faith anyway.

when you have done
all you have been commanded to do,
say "we are useless servants.
we have done no more than our duty."

luke 17:5–10

49

Apples on a Bright Fall Morning

MOST YEARS autumn comes in bushel baskets of extravagance and dumps herself on the floor of our lives. I should be tempted to say that she is too generous about it all, except how does one refuse such overabundance of life and color and field all harvested for our contentment. Most times her generosity catches me off guard, as if I will never learn to remember from year to year, and so it is for us all, I would suspect.

The Sunday comics reminded me of it a bit ahead of time this season as *Calvin & Hobbes* made their way from the civilization of their backyard and into the wilderness of their neighborhood. It was Calvin's six-year-old philosophizing to his tiger, Hobbes, that began the strip. "I wish I had more friends, but people are such jerks," is his observation on life. "If you can just get most people to ignore you and leave you alone, you're doing good. If you can find even one person you really like, you're lucky. And if that person can also stand *you*, you're *really* lucky." It is Hobbes, however, who sows a tiger's wisdom. "What if you find someone you can talk to while you eat apples on a bright fall morning?" And Calvin, like all of us who realize we've missed what should have been recognized, confesses, "Well, yeah...I suppose there's no point in getting greedy, is there?"

Perhaps it is not so much a matter of getting greedy, however, as it is a matter of recognizing that the miniature moments of life are not so miniature after all. Nor is it a matter of making sure we are grateful for them, for it seems that at such times gratitude is not something that is in need of being called forth as much as it is

153

our spontaneous response to discovering what is good in our lives, even to what is God in our lives.

So each year, like a miser unpacking in secret life's hoarded treasures in order to recount their worth, I go off to some hidden corner and unpack my memories lest, like Calvin, I miss (because of my greediness) what I should have recognized. I share them here with the thought that we may have them in common between us.

I find I'm thankful for the neighbor who yesterday risked a municipal fine and burned leaves in his backyard. The smell of burning leaves in autumn can equal that of bread baking in the oven.

I am thankful, too, for the year's simple gifts, at least the ones I find I can remember. The first day of Spring I remember because it came with such enthusiasm that I pulled my bike out of the basement and went for a marvelous ride down to the lake; and the dandelions too — I find I wait for them each year; and the barefoot walk I took through the dew on the grass; and the first apple of autumn; and the folk who said "I love you" to me, as well as those who kept on loving me though I hesitated saying "I love you" to them.

I am thankful for those summer days when the temperature reached over 90 — they were a marvelous excuse to do nothing and not feel guilty about it. Curiously enough, I find I'm also thankful for the mosquitoes — they remind we that life need not be big to make itself felt.

For the times the house was cold at night, I'm also grateful — the bed felt so much warmer then. And for all the check-out lines I stood in at the grocer's — I hated them but they reminded me that life needs to be slowed down.

In some strange way I find myself grateful as well for the toilet bowls I had to clean — they had their way of keeping life in perspective for me.

I'm thankful too for all the times that I could not pray. There were many such times, but they served to remind me that God is God and not I.

I find I can be thankful, too, for the problems life served up — they kept the days interesting and a challenge; and also for the times I suffered — they etched a wisdom upon my spirit no other process could have.

And finally I am grateful for those folks who made demands on me — they prevented me from becoming as selfish as I otherwise might have; and for those who disagreed with me — they forced me to recognize a different point of view and taught me the art of compromise as well.

Such is the basketful of gifts this autumn season spilled out upon my floor. I might have missed them had it not been for Calvin and Hobbes reminding me of what is important. But even more significantly, had it not been for the Samaritan leper who recognized what the other nine missed, I might have missed the fact that gratitude is one more face of God in a world of masks.

> *one of the ten,*
> *realizing that he had been cured,*
> *came back praising god in a loud voice.*
> *he threw himself on his face*
> *at the feet of jesus and spoke his praises.*
> *this man was a samaritan.*
>
> *luke 17:11–19*

50

Uncornered

Q UITE SIMPLY, it was the power of the question that caught me off guard — not the way it was asked nor why it was asked nor the circumstances surrounding it. It was simply the question itself — undoubtedly because I had never thought of it before. In fact, I was not even *asked* the question, nor was it even posed as a question. It was a comment tossed out between the two of us as part of a story, like a pebble kicked along during a casual walk — free to be kicked again or passed on by. Yet I couldn't escape asking it of myself.

John and I were in the car on our way to see a film. He was telling of a conversation with his sister about a course she was taking and of an assignment she had — to write on the primary quality of her mother that had been passed on to her. And that was where I found myself asking the question of myself. What troubled me, however, was that I had no answer — as much as I wanted one. I have much of my father in me — his penchant for public speaking seasoned with a touch of ham, his stubbornness, his mental thoroughness, his acceptance of life as he grew older. I see those in myself — easily and without much forethought. But of my mother's traits, I struggled to name one — as much as I wished I could name twenty. I have become who I am (as we all have, I suppose) without our choosing.

Life will have its own way — oftentimes in spite of our own best efforts — and what we do in the meantime may not even matter. Whom to marry, where to live, at which job we should bumble about — sometimes I wonder if any of it makes a difference or if

we do not become, in the end, the same folk one way or another.
And yet the truth is, we are also shaped by our choices. Perhaps
the more seasoned issue is the kind of heart with which we make
our choices.

I find older folks often rummaging about life in search of the
will of God — never the younger folk, though, and I wonder then
if such concern is something that comes with arthritis and gray
hair, or if it is rather a concern passing out of usage. If so, I would
not think it to be so tragic, for the will of God — or the kingdom
of God — seems to find its own place like water seeking its own
level. It need not be questioned and explored as if it were to be
created by us.

We can indeed question ourselves into a corner, or perhaps *be*
questioned as the case may be, and then discover that in reality
we have been questioned right out of the corner in which we have
been trying desperately to hide, questioned out into life without
any moorings except the trust that comes with that faith which says
it is all going somewhere. And whether or not we know where that
somewhere is matters little.

It would seem, indeed, that there is a kingdom reigning at the
heart of our efforts, a force insistent upon coming to be, and it is
present not only in us as individuals but also in us as communities
and as nations — pushing us and urging us to be what we have not
even dreamed possible. Like the parable of Jesus about the widow
knocking upon the judge's door in demand of justice, that force,
that kingdom, that spirit will not rest until it finds a home among
us. It is not so much that we must sort out the will of God from all
the other puzzle pieces, but rather we must simply let it reveal to
us the face of a God already present.

> *listen to what the corrupt judge has to say.*
> *will not god then do justice to his chosen*
> *who call out to him day and night?*
>
> *luke 18:1–8*

51

A Collection of Shadows

BY MOST STANDARDS OF MEASURE, on any other day it would have been a strange afternoon indeed. The porches at one end of the block had become fortresses for robed Arabs and Rambo militia in combat fatigues. The opposite end of the block found a royal princess holding court among a shuffling of bag ladies. And the in-between held a scattering of bumbling bees, strolling grapes, and skeletal remains of haunting lifetimes. Had it not been Halloween, it could well have been a smorgasbord of hallucinations or a Star Wars gathering of creatures from distant galaxies.

This year one of the local junior high schools forbad costumes with rubber masks of "Freddy" or "Jason" — both horror film characters carved from violence and sadism. I have often wondered about the relationship between our personalities and the costumes we wear for Halloween — whether the costumes we choose project our self-images or reveal our hungers. Is the ballerina someone graced and artful with an eye for beauty or someone strewn with clumsy and awkward drudgery in need of grace? Is the bloodthirsty ghoul a bully and a rogue or a gentle soul with a Freudian shadow? As in most of life, I suspect it is some of both — much like Jesus' story about the Pharisee and the tax collector who find themselves uncomfortably side by side in prayer, one trapped in his own goodness and the other in his own sin — each conspicuously framed by the other's history.

That unlikely duo is really each of us. We come with our own assorted goodness. We pray, we give to charity, we volunteer, we struggle to be honorable folk. Yet who of us would not blush if our full tale were told? We are a sifting of both — like dawn and dusk, each an unsortable mingling of darkness and light. However, it is not our goodness and virtue that save us, but rather it is our sin — opening us up to being filled by a merciful and gentle God. It is not our strength that proves to be the grace, but rather our weakness. It is the shadow that illumines the sun. It is the tax collected that pays the collector's debt.

This week's newspaper carried the story of Danny, a twelve-year-old victim of an alcoholic father who had entered recovery. Yet, as is so often the case, it was also the family who was in need of healing as well. Danny had come for treatment because he needed to be healed of his anger toward his father, an anger that showed itself in attacks of asthma with increasing frequency — to the point where Danny needed to begin curtailing his activities.

All Danny ever wanted was to be hugged by his dad, to be held and understood and protected. But his father never did or could satisfy that deep need of Danny's. Yet Danny found he hated his father in recovery more than he did while drinking because, as Danny told it, when his father drank he couldn't help being the father he was. Now in recovery, he was still distant and withheld his love from Danny — and he *could* help it. He did not have to be the way he continued to be.

One holiday season Danny watched his dad and his grand-father (his dad's dad) and noticed that his grandfather treated his son the way Danny's father treated Danny. And in that Danny realized why his dad was the way he was. As a result Danny decided not to wait until his dad would give him a hug. Instead, Danny began to hug his dad — "thirty-seven times over the past few months," he told Sharon Wegscheider-Cruse, his counselor and narrator of this story. He wanted to give his dad so many hugs that sooner or later his dad would realize what he had been given and that what he had been given was more than what he needed, and so he could then begin to give them away. And Danny wanted to be nearby to get the first one.

Like the tax collector, it was Danny's weakness and not his strength, his need for his father's love and not his independence, that saved him. It was that need that propelled him to hug his father again and again and again, and so unfold a love for his father. We need not fear our weaknesses or our sins. We need not fear our shadows. They are what save us and not our strengths.

And so it is, I suspect, that the costumes we wear in life do more to reveal our hungers than project our self-images, and perhaps that is the way it should be.

> *all he did was beat his breast and say,*
> *"o god, be merciful to me, a sinner."*
> *believe me,*
> *this man went home from the temple justified*
> *but the other did not.*
>
> *luke 18:9–14*

52

Gray Is Not Only a Color

BY THE TIME NOVEMBER TAKES ITS TURN UPON THE CALENDAR, it seems as if the year has pretty much emptied itself of life, having given over all of that on which it had gorged itself only weeks before. The trees, once dipped head first in lush greenery and stood on end to dry, now rattle in the hollow wind, their brilliance drained and dragged to earth. The fields, not so long ago salad bowls of tossed harvest, now lie gouged and rumpled. The sun has squandered its warmth, the day has cashed in its horde of light, and even the birds, it seems, have surrendered their song. Gray is not only a color.

In this season of emptied treasures, it is not so unusual, then, to find ourselves remembering those who emptied their lives for us and turned their backs on death with such love that it was almost as if they flaunted their faith at the specter itself. We remember them because they seemed to love without counting the cost. They scattered their love with abandon the way the wind scatters the crusty leaves — yet the memory of their love was gathered and pressed between the journal pages of our lives.

It seems we do not choose to do the remembering during these November days. We simply find ourselves about the business of doing it — remembering those who were emptied and, curiously, not those who were filled. And it all comes with a bit of a surprise — given that we humans put so much effort into filling our pockets and resumés and dreams. Perhaps of all the colors, then, gray should be most sacred — for it brings forth reflection and drapes life with a hue of holiness.

Until I was eight we lived above my grandparents in a small upstairs flat, though as I look back, I lived more of my days downstairs than upstairs. One of my most treasured places in those days was my grandfather's top dresser drawer in his bedroom. I am not sure what it was in that drawer that I found so enticing, but I can remember long times spent sorting through its riches. They all seem quite ordinary now: some insurance papers of one sort or another, torn envelopes with tissue paper windows, a gold pocket watch always asleep until I woke it, a wooden, black and white collapsible tape measure, broken at one end, some flat carpenter pencils left over from his trade, and much else, I am sure, though it all escapes me now.

Often I rummaged through those symbols of his life. What amazes me, however, as I think back is that he never once chided me for messing up his drawer — as indeed I am sure I did. He never pulled me out of that drawer, not even gently with a kind smile or laugh or tease. It is curious to me now that I should find those situations to be such symbols of his love squandered upon me. It may have been that it made little difference to him that I did what I did; yet for me it was a time when I shared in what it seemed was most personal to him. With a bit of presumption, I suppose, I find myself wondering in these days what people will remember as signs of love from my life.

we are god's children now;
what we shall later be has not yet come to light.
we know that when it comes to light
we shall be like him.

1 john 3:1–3
all saints

53

Life in the Trees

I WENT BACK LAST WEEK — back to when I was a child, back to a shrunken neighborhood, back to where we once hid our dares and double-dares, back to memories snagged on picket fences and caught in fruit trees ripe for climbing. Somewhere along the way most of us do go back at least once to the old neighborhood, to such a time before life began to unravel for us, when a bike ride to the corner was a journey to the end of the world. Then all we had was future and more of it than we would ever need, it seemed. Then the past was too meager to remember, and today was continually overstuffed with daydreams of what we would be.

The treasured world I had long ago buried there as a child I unearthed — only to find a cache of nostalgia and clichés. For an hour I walked the two worlds, bilocating generations of then and now. Every feeling was spliced together with both sadness and joy; every footstep carried me backward as well as forward; every gaze was not only settled in fog but also framed in sunlight. Living in two worlds tends to confuse what is real.

It was not so terribly different, I should think, than last Monday's teenagers who were lamenting the rigors of their state. That handful of youth had just come to realize that some unknown patron had paid the fare for their passage from childhood into adulthood — a trek much longer than is ever expected. They ridiculed the injustice of adult-priced admissions placed side by side with being told they were not old enough to own a driver's license. They pleaded for some logic to reconcile parent expectations for maturity with parental caution of immaturity. "When it's something they want, we're supposed to be adults. When it's something we want, we're only kids." Teenagers do wear a mix-matched pair of lives, often with each foot lived in a different story. They too find themselves living in two worlds, often muddling what is real.

Yet we all do it. We all do live in two worlds, seeking a way to live our shaded wants as well as our virtue — though we find each one diluting the other. It is all too real, like the fifty-year-old businessman forced to shave his values so that they can fit in the door frame of an unwelcome job he must keep in order to support his family. In the end he finds himself awkwardly at home in the two worlds of compromise and conviction, too embarrassed to admit the one and too committed to abandon the other. And living in the two, he confuses the real — for him and for us all.

Somewhere in life, then, all of us find ourselves touched by the shadow of Zacchaeus, that treed citizen of two worlds daring to live both. He lives compromised as a Roman tax agent, giving himself stature enough to see at least one world among his taller neighbors. Yet he lives with enough conviction that he can rebut his accusers and remind them and Jesus (and probably himself, as well) that he does give half of what he earns to the poor and does right wrongs four times over. And because of it all (or perhaps in spite of it all) Jesus spends the night in Zacchaeus's shadow while Zacchaeus spends it in Jesus' light — which is to say that probably neither of them did much sleeping that night.

And the struggle to discern which world is real? Well, it would appear that neither of them seemed to bother with it much, perhaps because together they discovered that the only real world is always the one of love.

> *you have mercy on all,*
> *because you can do all things;*
> *and you overlook the sins of men*
> *that they may repent.*
>
> *wisdom 11:22–12:1*

54

When We Die before We Die

DAYLIGHT SAVING TIME came to an end a few weeks back and with it an entire horizon of other lights as well — like apple stands along the highways, and Indian summer, and harvest moons, and that technicolor portion of autumn that makes the season worth having in the first place. Along with Halloween and trick-or-treating, the sealing off of Daylight Saving Time has become a season-ending ritual — as much as Labor Day and the opening of school is for summer and Easter for the season of winter.

The return of Standard Time brings about a different hue upon the hours. Mornings are suddenly brighter, as if pushed into daylight by some anxious timekeeper, and afternoons drag dim and weary so much sooner. It is as if life had skipped a beat during the night, and when the day awakes it is as if nothing is quite the same, as if during the night everything had been dismantled and then reassembled with some of the pieces missing. It is the same life except that it looks different. There is indeed more to turning back the clocks than turning back the clocks.

We take the process of settling in for winter a bit more in earnest after Daylight Saving Time ends. As the cold becomes more daring, teenagers move from street corners to shopping malls in search of a place to hang out. Children have more indoor play time as daylight seeps out through the cracks more quickly. Bikes are brought down to the basement, storm windows are hung, and preparations are begun for the season of family feasts. Life does settle in, and how we live the winter is so different.

Yet the turn of the seasons and its dismantling and reassembling of our lives is but an echo of a much deeper process continually at play within the heart of who we are. We ourselves are dismantled and reassembled.

Lynn Caine entitled her book *Widow* as she described the remaking of her life after the death of her husband, Martin.

> Today I carry the scars of my bitter grief . . . marks of my fight to attain an identity of my own. I owe the person I am today to Martin's death. If he had not died, I am sure I would have lived happily ever after as a twentieth century child wife never knowing what I was missing.
>
> But today I am someone else. I am stronger, more independent. I have more understanding, more sympathy. A different perspective. I have a quiet love for Martin. I have passionate, poignant memories of him. He will always be part of me.
>
> But Martin is dead. And I am a different woman. And the next time I love, if ever I do, it will be a different man, a different love.
>
> Frightening.
>
> But so is life. And wonderful.*

The truth of the matter is that the white-robed prophet of snickered doom who proclaims that the end is near is right — only the end comes before the end and usually more than once. Our lives do collapse in such cosmic ways that not one stone is left upon another. The end may come with the premature death of someone we love as it did for Lynn Caine, or it may come with premature illness for ourselves. But it may also take the shape of an unexpected pregnancy in midlife or confrontation of a life collapsed by addiction. Or it may happen slowly as we surrender passion or enthusiasm or dreams or youth, like color faded by sunlight yet never noticed till the past in uncovered, and suddenly we realize the color of life is no color at all.

Again and again our lives are dismantled and then reassembled, and sometimes those transitions come with more violence than the end of the world we have come to dread. Indeed, there we come to recognize that we have been put to death, forced to confess that whatever the future, it will not be of our own making. Then we

---

*Lynn Caine, *Widow* (New York: Wm. Morrow & Co., Inc., 1974), 222.

see that we have been refashioned, recreated from nothing into a marvelously new creation — just like the first time. It is the story of the divine phoenix rising from the ashes, lived by every human being, and understood by every sister and brother who lives in Christ Jesus.

> *some were speaking of how the temple was adorned....*
> *jesus said,*
> *"these things you are contemplating —*
> *the day will come*
> *when not one stone will be left upon another,*
> *but it will all be torn down....*
> *you will be delivered up ...,*
> *yet not a hair of your head will be harmed.*
> *by patient endurance*
> *you will save your lives."*
>
> *luke 21:5–19*